MW01700583

"Doug Peacock's long-awaited *Walking It Off* instructs us once more why Doug Peacock is viewed as the ethical benchmark for any discussions or philosophy regarding the remnant American wilderness, and our society's relationship to that wildness. His is a singular and heroic life comprised not just of words and literature, but of deeds. Some days I have the fear that Doug Peacock stands nearly alone in this country as antidote to the strange aggression or, perhaps worse, numbness, that visits too many of us these days when we gaze upon our last wildlands, and the value and lessons such lands hold for a country's innate potential for true greatness. This book is a fitting companion to his earlier classic, *Grizzly Years*: please read them both, read it all."

—Rick Bass, *The Ninemile Wolves*

"Take this powerful, life-changing walk with Doug Peacock. He is a frontiersman, a philosopher, and a great guru of the mountains. We walk alone so much in this world. But no longer."

—Gerry Spence, *How to Argue and Win Every Time*

"Doug Peacock is a direct literary descendant of Thoreau, with a few genes from Audubon and his mentor, Edward Abbey, thrown in for good measure. His response to the natural world is visceral, intellectual and spiritual at the same time. In this book, he writes about it beautifully, in prose that begs favorable comparison to the best of Peter Matthiessen. Too many modern environmentalists, in their attempt to spare our diminishing wildlands from our rapacious culture, cite their utilitarian and economic value. *Walking It Off* shows that wilderness, like a great work of art, possesses an intrinsic value in its power to restore, to revitalize, to heal the stricken soul. His meditations on war and wilderness are painfully apt today, with America fighting new battles abroad, led by an administration that seems to be at war with wilderness at home.

—Phil Caputo, *Pulitzer Prize winner*

"Doug Peacock's *Walking It Off* is an extraordinary and durable book. Frankly, Peacock's life makes nearly all of the environmental movement look like an upper class bridge tournament. In *Walking It Off*, you have the heart and soul, more exactly the blood and guts, of a man who has given his life in defense of nature, intermixed with the story of his dearest friend and mentor, Ed Abbey."

—Jim Harrison, *Legends of the Fall*

"Doug Peacock is an iconic figure, a secular prophet, in the wildass American West. His voice is important, angry, humane, and unique. He's also our best living connection to another essential American crank: the late Edward Abbey. This wonderful book tells the story of their consequential friendship, and much more."

—David Quammen, *Song of the Dodos*

"At a time when we don't know who to believe or what to believe, when nothing around us feels trustworthy, Doug Peacock's book, *Walking It Off*, arrives as a talisman of truth. We need his empathy. We are hungry for his honest accounting and we are inspired by his compassionate response to the world. But what moves me most about Doug Peacock is his willingness to be vulnerable—why we both laugh and cry through his stories. This is what we are missing—an ethical path. Doug Peacock is a humble warrior, fearless and honest, with a heart as big as the wild country he loves. His life is his work. He continues to grow. That he has chosen to put his words on the page with the patience and struggle it requires of him is another act of his signature courage and endurance. As long as we have heroes like Doug Peacock in America—who are willing to stand up to our government when it lies, who can call for an end to the violence on America's wildlands, and who speak from the shattered experience of being a veteran of war—we can still believe in the strength of words like patriotism, freedom, and sacrifice."

—Terry Tempest Williams, *The Open Space of Democracy*

"An intense, personal, and very painful tribute to a thorny friendship and its shared vision of the stunted modern values that waste and desecrate our country's land and life; appropriately, the book is woven on a background of bloody expeditionary wars in Asia that future Americans will judge useless—indeed senseless."

—Peter Matthiessen, *The Snow Leopard*

"I'm crazy for this book, its oxygenic prose, its fidelities, The desert's hard to conjure, it's so cruel and other, but Peacock's loving and respectful comprehension of it seems complete. It takes a wild heart to be one with the wildest places and this is one big true and wild heart walking here."

—Joy Williams, *Ill Nature*

WALKING IT OFF

EASTERN WASHINGTON UNIVERSITY PRESS

WALKING IT OFF

A VETERAN'S CHRONICLE OF WAR AND WILDERNESS

DOUG PEACOCK

© 2005 by Doug Peacock. All rights reserved.
Printed in the United States of America

10 09 08 07 06 05   5 4 3 2 1

Design by A.E. Grey.

Cover photo credits Top: US soldiers participating in Operation Thayer II, Vietnam by Kyoichi Sawada. (#U1658510 © Bettman/Corbis). Bottom: Rock formation in the Arizona desert (#imh01026031 © gettyimages).

This book is printed on 50% post-consumer waste recycled paper.

The stories about Nepal and Abbey's burial have been previously published in the August 1997 issue of *Outside Magazine;* that about Nepal also in *Meanderings, Voices from the Round River.*

Library of Congress Cataloging-in-Publication Data

Peacock, Doug.
Walking it off : a veteran's chronicle of war and wilderness / Doug Peacock.
p. cm.
ISBN 0-910055-99-8 (pbk. : alk. paper)
1. Peacock, Doug. 2. Naturalists—United States—Biography. 3. Peacock, Doug—Journeys—West (U.S.) 4. Environmentalists—United States—Biography. 5. Vietnamese Conflict, 1961-1975—Veterans—United States—Biography. 6. Post-traumatic stress disorder—Patients—United States—Biography. 7. Abbey, Edward, 1927-—Friends and associates. 8. West (U.S.)—History. I. Title.
QH31.P24A3 2005
508'.092—dc22

2005021503

Eastern Washington University Press
Cheney and Spokane, Washington

For Colin, Laurel, Kathryn

And in memoriam
Marion E. Peacock

CONTENTS

ACKNOWLEDGEMENTS

I am deeply indebted to the following individuals and groups for their support and assistance:

Clarke Abbey, Rick Bass, Marc Beaudin, Carl Brandt, Jeff and Susan Bridges, Russell Chatham, Malinda and Yvon Chouinard, Mike Cochran, Tom Cox, Bob Datilla, The Foundation for Deep Ecology, Sid Gustafson, Greg Hall, Jim and Linda Harrison, Christopher Howell, Greg Keeler, Margo Kidder, John and Hilary Klein, Gary Kneip, Mike and Pam Hausman, Heather Kilpatrick, John W. Jones (Jonesy), Rust Hills, Island Press, Jack Macrae, Bud Lucas, Peter Matthiessen, Preston Maring, Dr. James A. Meyer, Craig Mielke, Beth McIntosh, Rod MacIver, Rod Mondt, Phil Morton, Mark and Linda Papworth, Phyllis Peacock, Steve and Susan Prescott, Round River Conservation Studies, Dr. H. Russell Sampley, Trent and Dennis Sizemore, Doug and Anne Stanton, Doug and Lynne Seus, Dan Sullivan, Joy Williams and Terry Tempest Williams

I send a deep well of love and thanks to Andrea Peacock for her courage, patience and endurance in weathering the storm.

My earnest respect and appreciation goes out to all those who insisted that I revisit this work. Without your passionate encouragement, this book would not have been published. I owe you an explanation.

WALKING IT OFF

NEPAL: DHAULAGIRI

High in the shadow of Dhaulagiri they are bleeding the yaks. Two Tibetans hold the curved horns of the shaggy beast and a third man uses a wooden bowl to catch the bright red blood that pulses and spills out a hole in the yak's neck. The big oxen struggles to escape the hobbles binding its legs, then quiets and stands peacefully, submitting to its fate; the Tibetans believe that bleeding a liter or two of blood from a mature animal's throat makes the yak stronger and that drinking yak blood cures humans of intestinal ailments.

Across the deepest valley in the world the monsoon clouds billow, then part, revealing immaculate snowfields falling off the western shoulder of Annapurna. These high summer pastures lie slightly above the tree line at about 14,000 feet. Clumps of dwarf juniper cling to the hillside and a sparse cover of late summer grasses carpet the gentler slopes. The clouds drift in and out, now uncovering a huge ice field on the steep northern slope of Nilgiri. The light is crystalline.

I am here with two friends, biologist Dennis Sizemore and British climber Alan Burgess. We are the only Westerners. The other four are Sherpas, a local man from the village of Marfa six thousand feet below, and three young men from the Makalu area west of Everest whom Al has hired as porters. It is the off-season for trekking and these people are the last humans we expect to see as we climb on up to the high valleys north of Dhaulagiri. We want to explore this area for wild sheep and goats, snow leopards, wolves, and maybe bears and yetis. These valleys fall off into deep gorges and are separated by high peaks but with a bit of technical scrambling you can get from one to the next and follow them north all the way to Tibet. We have heard more Himalayan blue sheep live in these wild basins between Dolpo and Mustang than in any other part of Nepal. There may also be rare Marco Polo sheep and wolves in the area. Al's friend Bhahti, who runs a teahouse in Marfa and who accompanied Alan to the summit of Dhaulagiri, has seen the *tracks of four different snow leopard in Hidden Valley, which lies just above us, beyond the 17,000 foot pass.*

If you glance at a map of Nepal (which is all I did before going there) you will see that the more or less uniformly spaced village names thin out or disappear when you reach the rain shadow of Dhaulagiri, in the empty borderland between Dolpo and Mustang. This land runs north-northeast in the lee of Dhaulagiri over the high plateaus of the Mustang Himal into Chinese-occupied Tibet. It is uninhabited high country, mostly 16,000 to 19,000 feet, generally above the range of trees but with alpine plant communities that support wild goat and sheep. Accordingly, our journey will not be the usual ecotour or ethnographic trek; we plan to leave the trails and villages behind and travel without permits into forbidden and uninhabited country.

I came here in my fifties to walk myself into good health: to walk off the roll of belly fat around my middle-aged gut, to walk away from war, to walk up and on in defiance of my hereditary gift of high cholesterol and blood pressure into a dimly perceived better world and maybe a new beginning. I wanted more life and more out of the living I had left.

To our backs, the dark gorge of the Kaligandaki slices a 10,000-foot swath between the Dhaulagiri and Annapurna himals; fresh snow has softened the rugged face of Nilgiri and Khangshar Kang. Now the last sunlight irradiates the high snowfields, which hold their brilliance long after the sun sets. I watch the inner flush of the mountains against the dark sky, a dull pearly luminosity that glows until the stars come out.

During the night I lie in my tent with a mild altitude headache and nurse a chronic cough that has kept me awake much of the past two months. The distant roar of another avalanche off Dhaulagiri rolls over the foothills and down the valley. I listen to the silence that follows then rummage through my backpack and dig out two codeine tablets to suppress the cough. I smile as I remember how my old friend, the anarchist writer Ed Abbey—after he had to quit drinking—looked forward to his legal codeine fix each evening in the year before he bled to death from ruptured veins in his throat.

Ed passed on to me a great tool for survival. He died dreaming of "great walks." I was in my forties then and began to realize that I too wasn't going to be around forever so I'd better take those walks and trips while I still could. Not long after Ed died, I began to travel with deliberation, walking beyond the familiar and outside the bounds of my own culture.

I followed the Abbey method (less a technique for thought and meditation than an opportunity for new possibilities and combinations): go to the wildest place you can find, alone if possible, open your mind, and walk. The journey that led me here began on a desert island in Mexico just before Abbey died. I attended that death, clinging tightly to my funeral duties. After burying Ed, weary from the death watch, I disappeared into the canyon country of southern Utah that Abbey had so loved, searching for a sign. Even years later, my Vietnam experience returning with a fury, my domestic life completely unraveling, I used old Ed's experience as a guide, descending into the rugged barrancas of the Tarahumara Indians in Mexico's Sierra Madres, visiting native people living on the corners of the continent, places Abbey had also visited, seeking insight. That search has taken me back to Asia for the first time since my days as a Green Beret medic in Vietnam, to the salmon rivers at the edge of Siberia, following tiger tracks along the Sea of Japan, and here to the Himalayas. In all these travels I intend to walk off the beaten paths, hike off the trails, bushwhacking in body and mind to see the world anew—it was the way I decided to live the rest of my life. I needed to get out in order to look back in. I believed that walking off my stale entrenched life and into a new beginning could succeed no matter what my age, that it had everything to do with living well each day. Ed's death was a wake-up call, and since his death I lived with a growing sense that my life was racing toward metamorphosis, maybe even death, hurtling into the fires of transformation.

By morning a light snow covers the ground down to about 17,000 feet, just above my tent. Snow partridges cluck on a nearby ridgeline then flush, disappearing into a gully. We leave Kalipani and start up the faint trail, crossing a few patches of steep snow and treacherous scree. Pemba, the head Sherpa, uses his knife to cut steps in the hard snow of the gullies. I gasp in the thin air, my mind fuzzy, walking in a mental and literal fog that hangs in the passes and drifts down the trail. After about an hour, I seem to get a second wind. My mind slowly clears. By 16,000 feet I feel great, like a bull yak, striding with ease up toward a bench below the pass. Above, the grasses disappear and a landscape of scree and bedrock closes in on all horizons. On the steep path approaching 17,000 feet, I wonder how old Ed would have fared here. He felt weak (he was low on blood) on his last trips to our beloved Cabeza Prieta desert the winter before he died. He knew that with esophageal varices he was living under a death sentence (the medical book said: "Esophageal varices are a grave prognostic sign; about 60% succumb to death within a year"), and he thought "one's death should mean something." By the time Abbey died he had the clearest eyes I ever encountered—an image that still haunts me.

I saw then that being willing to die, prepared to die, was not the same as being prepared for death. Death is no stranger to me; I lost many a comrade on the road that brought me here. For over three decades, I had flirted with death, even courted it. I lived on the edge in Vietnam and later for more than a decade with grizzlies, on snow-covered mountains and raging rivers or, as often as I could, among polar bears, jaguars, and tigers. Yet, I think somehow Ed's death is the closest I may get, until my own turn comes around. With Ed, I walked a long way into death. I saw in those eyes another universe; he died so well. Living among a people for whom death often arrives as an unexpected surprise, his dying was the bravest and finest of all the gifts he gave me.

High above, an Egyptian vulture soars over the glacial valley. I hold my binoculars on the bird and, for a minute, fly with the white buzzard, up through the monsoon clouds, above the great glaciers and snowfields across the world toward the topography of my own days, a desert island in the Sea of Cortez.

1 ISLA TIBURÓN

A cool morning breeze from Tiburón Island raced across the saltwater strait known as the Infernillo, "The Little Hell." I wondered if the weather might be changing. Winter in northern Mexico tended to pass in large blocks of sunshine interrupted by three-day blows that rattled the soul. Ahead, a line of brown pelicans rode a crest of wave passing across the bow of our open boat. In the gray distance, I could see big cardon and organ pipe cactus on uninhabited Isla Tiburón. Two hundred miles to the north a friend was dying in Tucson, where I had left two children and an unhappy wife. I knew that didn't sound good but I couldn't help myself.

The friend was of course Edward Abbey, a well-known writer in this part of the country. He agreed this potentially marriage-wrecking trip was worth the risk. Coming here to Tiburón Island was an idea the two of us had dreamed up long ago around a desert campfire, the night we charted our greatest unfulfilled wild adventures in a place called the Cabeza Prieta. Now I was going without him.

The soul also needs nourishing. Like Abbey and other friends, I was one of those who could not live without wild country. Even today, the wilderness experience remains a timeless way of seeking and, for some, a true and modern addiction.

To the east, rising out of the foothills of the Sierra Madre, the desert sun broke free of thin morning clouds. From the boat, it was hard to remember this was one of the driest regions in North America. The sea was still relatively calm; later, around midday, the winter chop would kick up. We motored up the coast past Isla Alcatraz, a local landmark on the mid-eastern seaboard of the Sea of Cortez. The open panga snaked into a belt of surf at the opening of the strait where strong tides from the narrows collided with ocean breakers.

I was traveling with three friends and their two children who had flown out from central California. This island off the Sonoran

Coast of Mexico's Gulf of California was the wildest spot I could visit without taking a complete powder on my responsibilities.

But the trip to Tiburón was impossible to pass up—it was not only as wild as I could get, it was also as far as I felt I could comfortably range at the time, since Abbey's health had dramatically declined: I was afraid he might die before I got back to Tucson, and I had promised to be there at the end.

We turned west into the strait, passing a gray whale and her calf halfway through the Infernillo. Far ahead the channel narrowed around Punta Chueca and Estero Santa Rosa, one of Abbey's favorite camping areas on the mainland Sonoran coast. Mine too. In the two decades Ed and I had known each other, we had gazed at Tiburón countless times, looking west across the straits of the Infernillo, itching to explore its untrammeled hills and valleys, its giant cactus forests and exotic plants and animals. The island remained one place we never had time to see.

It was love of the wilderness—and the need to protect it—that had brought the two of us together twenty years before. We had become friends, shared jobs, camped out, and traveled together. Ed, who was fifteen years older, became a guide in my own life, though experience cut both ways. The wild was what we held in common.

Riding in the bow of the panga, it suddenly occurred to me, and with startling lucidity, that Ed Abbey was really going to die this time. Until that moment, I hadn't quite believed it. He had been sick a long time, nearly five years, but in the past month he had seemed increasingly resigned, alternately cranky and peaceful with a raw humor, which I believed meant he was ready to go.

Pods of bottle-nosed and common dolphin snorkeled by and sea lions fed all around us. We went by a little island that looked like a porcupine covered with quills of giant cardon cactus, arriving off the southern tip of Tiburón at midday of February 18th.

Ed Abbey considered Tiburón ("shark" in Spanish) one of the last great wild places in all of cactus country; the fact that it is an island in one of the richest regions of the Sea of Cortez and that this island, though now abandoned, had been occupied by the Seri Indians and their prehistoric ancestors for some eight thousand years, just added to its mystery and allure. He yearned to explore the jagged Sierra Kunkaak, or the peaks of the Sierra Menor, with the great interior valley lying between the two—a broad bajada studded with cardon and pitaya, home to the densest population of mule deer remaining in the cactus forests of Sonora and Arizona.

This valley was also home to the last Seri band to come in from the wilderness, the last group of holdouts, who fiercely resisted the Spanish and the Mexican Army, refusing to come in to the missions and towns to accept the questionable advantages of Christianity and agriculture (facts that were not lost on Ed Abbey). To him, the Seris were the embodiment of wild resistance, their desert island a last refuge of freedom.

I jumped off the bow of the panga and helped beach the boat. Within minutes we had unloaded our gear and made camp in a cove at the bottom of a sandy wash dumping into the sea from the desert above. I trudged a hundred yards back up the wash to pitch my tent, away from the others. The Mexican fisherman we had hired to ferry us out started back to Old Kino Bay; he would return for us in six days. I walked down the coarse winter beach to grab a bit of solitude. I wanted very much to believe that a kind of ancient wisdom resided in the land itself, especially in places like Tiburón, haunted with the ghosts of generations of hunters and warriors.

Tiburón was unlike the other gulf islands, botanically complex and unfamiliar, different from the everyday cactus forest country of Arizona. It felt non-Western, as strange as Mars in its historical tribal cultural affiliations, its archeology unknown. Largest of the gulf islands in terms of area, Tiburón had drinking water, which made it habitable, though some years it might not rain at all. The average was probably four or five inches annually, and came mostly during summer monsoons and occasional tropical chubascos. Still, more than three hundred species of vascular plants grew there, and the island had a large number of big mammals, especially deer, which might account for the eight thousand years of human occupation.

The next morning, from the headland above our camp, I watched spouts of fin whales far out in the morning calm. I began my exploration of the island by looping east along the coast, then back up the Arroyo Sauzal where it was rumored there was permanent water. The bottoms of the washes, brushy with wolfberry, ironwood, and acacia thorn bushes, swarmed with songbirds. Bright cardinals and pyrrhuloxias perched in ocotillo and mockingbirds mimicked a small songbird, probably a yellow-green vireo, which sang a repetitious song of bird life, echoed every several seconds from a nearby roost in a thicket of palo verde.

I climbed up the wash through granodiorite boulders to a low saddle. At the pass, I sat down on a round rock and looked back; a wedge of blue ocean shimmered beyond the desert valley. I could still hear the vireo singing away, expending energy far in excess of any function or reward I could imagine; the optimism of this pocket-sized, Sisyphean insect-eater was a definitive refutation of bird suicide.

Abbey and I were having our last big squabble over this very issue. Just before I left Tucson to come down here, we had a nasty quarrel over a .357 Magnum pistol. It was a serious disagreement, and I wasn't sure I was doing the right thing. The gun was Ed's. He had brought the pistol and a pair of muddy boots over to my house one day when I wasn't around and hid them in my garage. The boots and gun had been involved in some sort of monkey wrenching. Although I didn't need or want to know exactly what, I would expect it had something to do with the developer's heavy equipment that was clear-cutting the desert behind Ed's house. That Ed would hide felonious incriminating evidence at my place sounds worse than it really was. The fact that he was actively engaging in mischief right up to the end was something I approved of and supported. The row—our fight—was over the .357; last month, I had appropriated the gun and sent it away. Other guns were available but he wanted this one and was justly angry. It was our last big argument and the only time in our friendship I ever passed judgment and went against his wishes.

The issue was, of course, the right to an end. Thinking about suicide is not the same as being on the trail of the real thing. Ed was clear-minded on the subject, valuing the notion of suicide apart from the collateral damage the actual deed inflicts on survivors. Contemplating ending one's life can be beneficial, providing a sense of control over a life-threatening disease, a new lease on the future. He thought that "like sex and alcohol, the ready availability of suicide was one of life's basic consolations."

When our friend (my best friends at that time were both named Ed) Ed Gage cured his pain with a shotgun, I was too young to know how deep the darkness of depression could get. I looked for scapegoats and excuses: those bastard primal scream therapists in Santa Monica who had him on 300 mg of Thorazine per day; Gage's break up with a long-term girlfriend. Gage conned me with a phone call saying he was doing great, but I've never forgotten that I didn't make a call back to him that day he decided to buy the shotgun and shells. His suicide note, found ten days later with his body in the back of his camper, said he was sorry for his friends but he just couldn't stand the pain anymore. I thought then there must have been more to it. But I was wrong.

Gage killed himself because the incomprehensible pain of his depression was so hopeless that oblivion was his only way out. Abbey had had his own bouts with "melancholia" throughout his adult life, the depths of which I would later discover on a weeklong walk across the Cabeza Prieta. It would take me a quarter of a century to admit that the cluster of symptoms, which I attributed to a mere winter seasonal affliction (the onset of which I date from the Tet Offensive), were mostly a matter of ordinary depression.

The notion of being able to take one's own life had been important in my own world; I wrote a book about grizzly bears in part to disclose why I had declined to slip out life's back door. Since Vietnam, suicide had traveled with me like a spare canteen. But after the birth of my daughter, I knew I couldn't drink from it. For courage, I flippantly formulated that you might take a bad man with you. That is, if you knew you were going to die, or if life became so unsatisfactory you didn't care to go on, why not do something wonderfully bold, courageous, or reckless like taking out the dictator, executioner, or Nazi of your choosing. Ed Abbey looked forward to the day "when somebody with a terminal disease (such as life) is going to strap a load of TNT around his waist and go down into the bowels of Glen Canyon dam and blow that ugly thing to smithereens. That would be a good way to go."

Yet in the end, my friends and acquaintances who had opted for suicide were so defeated by the lives they were leaving behind that they no longer cared about doing worldly good.

It's uncanny when in a relationship—a friendship between two men in this case—the brotherhood experiences a growth spurt and surges to a deeper or more mature plane. There had always been a paternalistic edge to our friendship; Ed was 15 years older and for years I seemed arrested in lingering adolescence, all of which encouraged the imbalance. But on the note sounded over the Magnum pistol, the paternalism began to rapidly erode.

The reason I wouldn't give the gun back had to do with our four children, my boy and girl and Ed's most recent son and daughter, who were all about the same age and close friends. It had been a coincidence that both of us would start families at the same time, my first and for Ed, the wife and children who would finally provide the domestic tranquility he had never quite managed to enjoy. I knew we all had reason to want to hang around. I also knew that Ed had been bleeding and was low on blood, that this had affected his judgment. Medically, his case wasn't hopeless, though Ed was too stubborn to seriously entertain high-tech surgical intervention. I was worried about the kids, about inflicting lasting damage. At the same time, I considered my act of precluding Ed's only simple alternative to a potentially miserable and vile death just steps away from unforgivable cruelty.

That evening I returned to camp and settled in with my companions. It was great to have children along. It had been a mistake not to bring my own son and daughter. I had thought them too young, and now realized they would have loved it, and would have helped anchor my attention. As it was, I tried to be a decent companion but my mind was somewhere else. These friends were leaders of the American conservation movement—Rick Ridgeway, a world-famous mountaineer, and Yvon Chouinard, the owner of an international outdoor clothing company—and among the most important people to me outside my immediate family, yet I wasn't quite there. My life was so buried in transition that I felt incapable of living in the present, the only authenticity I had ever coveted. These trips were supposed to bring out the best in me, but this time, in the beginning, it wasn't working.

We had all brought our daily catch to the fire: a couple dozen turban snails gathered from below the lowest low-tide mark, a factor important in how they taste; and half a dozen pound-sized spotted sea bass—superior food, my friends argued, to the trigger fish I had hooked from the rocks on orange marabou flies. We boiled up the turban snails while I prepared a sauce of lemon, olive oil, garlic, and fresh oregano. We pried off the operculum with our knives and dipped the escargot in the sauce.

My buddy Rick, who had been on the first American team to summit K-2, had climbed the face of the granodiorite headland in the afternoon and paused halfway up when a peregrine falcon complained loudly above him. He looked back down; 30 yards out from the foot of the cliff was a big flat rock. On either side of the rock, two killer whales paused, facing in. From the ocean side, a huge male orca rose out of the sea and landed on top of the flat rock, two-thirds of his giant body hanging out of the water, eyes rolling from side to side, looking for sea lions. My friend, one of the last great American adventurers, called the image quintessential.

Perhaps inspired by his vision, that night I dreamed a dangerously erotic dream (a reoccurring theme) of a female jaguar that left me with a strange openness. The same sort of vulnerability often surfaced after close encounters with grizzlies. I fed off danger, crisis, and tended to create disasters when domestic life was going well, becoming the kind of asshole for which there are modern psychiatric names. This addiction to risk could separate you from your own kind, even the people closest in your life.

Hostility, generally expecting the worst from people, had been my general approach to life since Vietnam. This attitude colored my friendship with Ed and was further complicated by his creation of the fictional personality of ex-Green Beret medic George Washington Hayduke, the hairy, beer-swilling main character of *The Monkey Wrench Gang*, a comic hero belied by the extreme social and personal limitations of a damaged war veteran, a man loosely based on the younger Doug Peacock. There may be numerous ways to characterize a friendship of a volatile, unformed youth (a man who appeared to be an angry force of nature) with an older, successful, better educated and generally more sophisticated man, but I return to the paternalistic model because much of the friction was due to a father–son-like relationship. The anger of the son kept the friendship arrested in this imbalance and anchored in a limited machismo code.

Once Ed published *The Monkey Wrench Gang* in 1975 and it sold half a million copies, the character of Hayduke became famous in a lowbrow sort of way. "Hayduke Lives" was scribbled on bathroom walls in bars throughout the American West. This was hardly an endorsement of excellence, nor flattery of any variety; Hayduke, as a representation of Peacock, was a one-dimensional dolt. A mutual acquaintance of both myself and Abbey once remarked, in reference to the modeling of Hayduke on Peacock: "Friends don't do that to each other," meaning that in some way Ed was abusing our friendship. This is correct, in that the portrayal of George Washington Hayduke reflected the adolescent, wayward son, not the maturing friend. To the extent I was seduced by the hype of George Washington Hayduke (and to a degree, I believe I was), I succumbed even more to the anger. I plead guilty to all charges.

On the other hand, Abbey probably did me a favor in creating a caricature of myself whose dim psyche I could penetrate when my own seemed off-limits; Ed painted the ex-Green Beret Hayduke, with precise brushstrokes, as caught in an emotional backwater, a backwater out of which I wanted to swim. The only thing worse than reading your own press was becoming someone else's fiction.

The next day I packed up for a full day of exploration. I climbed north over a low pass through giant cactus and elephant trees, then turned east through several miles of rolling hills, and I entered a broad valley that stretched down to the sea. It was dominated by an arroyo that reached back into the mountains and became a brushy canyon thick with thorny vegetation. That was where the water would be.

Wolfberry and catclaw acacia tugged at my clothes as I followed a deer trail into the valley bottom. The wash grew thick with canyon ragweed, desert lavender, bumelia trees, burro bush, dogbane, and many shrubs I didn't recognize. I passed several sets of deer antlers bleaching on the alluvial soil. I saw tracks of a small cat of 15 pounds or so. Most of the sets of mule deer antlers on Tiburón that I had seen were small. Mountain lions probably didn't live here, though I wasn't certain of this.

On a bench just above the big wash was a stone metate, a grinding bowl with the mono, or grinder, still in it. I looked around: piles of murex, turban snails and their operculum (the same species we had eaten back at camp with the garlic and oregano sauce), glycymeris, and other clam and oyster shells lay in heaps everywhere; in between, broken and smaller chione shells littered the ground, along with flakes of dacite and obsidian and lots of broken pottery. It was a big archeological site, about a mile from the ocean, not far, no doubt, from fresh water just up the brushy canyon. I found more metates with the monos in them, ready to go, as if the people had planned on returning. These ancient sorts of grinding tools had been used for maybe six thousand years so it was impossible to tell how old they were. Amid the debris were occasional arrowpoints, egg-shell pottery, and thicker potsherds with red lines painted on them. I found several gaming disks of pottery and one turtle-like figurine. Finally, I found two iron arrowheads, triangular in shape and without stems, possibly hammered out of nails or barrel hoops.

This site had been occupied for a long time, perhaps as far back as several thousand years, and certainly, as evidenced by the iron points, up until recent times. The entire history of a people lay here, including the story of European conquest, of great interest to Ed, who saw Tiburon Island as an archetypical homeland for tribal people. The way in which Spanish military had dealt with the Seris became the deadly model later transported north and put into practice by other European immigrants, our ancestors.

That the Seri Indians didn't currently live there wasn't important. It was the land that counted. The land could still share its tribal lessons, especially if you took the effort to learn its history and cultural affiliations. Abbey noted a magical quality about the place. I had counted on this.

The Seris were one of only two Mexican tribes who, at the time of the conquest, were hunters and gatherers instead of farmers. The Indians were initially friendly to the Spaniards and missionaries who visited their homeland; in 1748, however, the Spanish summarily deported the women of 80 Seri families to

Guatemala and elsewhere in New Spain where they were sold into slavery, or worse, and were never again seen by their families. The Seri men warned the missionaries, whom they did not want to harm, then, quite naturally went on the attack. The subsequent murderous response of the Spanish turned the Seri into marauding raiders, whose warlike reputation in this part of the world was equaled only by the Apaches. Seri Indians were hunted down and slaughtered, wherever the Spanish could find them, for the next century and a half. In return, the natives routinely ambushed parties traveling the road between Hermosillo and Guaymas and hunted cattle—known elsewhere to the Indian as "slow elk"—that grazed alongside the deer and rabbits, whenever the chance presented.

Ed Abbey admired these cow killers, these independent warrior people. In particular, he loved the stories of Seris burying their enemies up to their necks in anthills. He was also fond of the tales of cannibalism (though these were mostly bullshit), of Seris boiling missionaries in huge ollos then passing out the best pieces of meat according to an elaborate system based on kinship lines, a common distribution ethic among subsistence hunters of the desert (whereby your mother's brother's daughter's husband gets the first cut, a prime round of thigh of large Jesuit).

Of course, by the time of my sojourn on Tiburón the surviving Seri settled in villages and lived by selling ironwood carvings to tourists. To Abbey, however, these last Seris, merely by virtue of their survivorship, embodied the tribal resistance against the onslaught of industrial and agrarian technologies. He admired their spunk, as he had the Aborigines' when he visited Australia or the Tarahumara Indians of the great barrancas of the Sierra Madre. The wilderness is vanishing, he said, and the next to go will be the last primitive tribes, the traditional cultures. "Seri" means "the wild people." It was amazing that people so different from us still lived that close to Tucson.

Days passed. I watched the sunrise over the Sea of Cortez, the islands of Datil and Esteban shape-shifting, seeming to float on the seamless surface of sky and ocean. Each day we explored this nearly uninhabited island and lived off fish and moon snails served with garlic and oregano sauces. In the evenings we gathered by the campfire and shared our various harvests.

I decided to pack up enough gear for an overnight trip into the interior. I wanted to bushwhack east across to the Infernillo channel, though there was a three-man detachment of soldiers on the coast south of there I'd have to sneak by. The three soldiers lived in a shack on the southern coast for the declared purpose of protecting Tiburón from Seri or Mexican deer poachers. The story was that these three poor soldiers had fallen asleep while guarding a bank in Mexico City and that bank robbers had slipped past them, making off with the loot while the boys were slumbering. Their punishment was this forlorn outpost in the blistering summer heat of Tiburón.

I knew that throughout the previous 300 years, the Seri had occupied Tiburón more or less continually. In the decades that followed the deportation of the Seri women in 1748, only Tiburón remained a haven for the tribe, and even this sanctuary was invaded in 1750 by an expedition of 75 Spanish soldiers and some 400 Upper Pimas who swept through the entire Seri territory, killing only a handful of Seris, mostly women. The great majority of Seri at that time retreated to the rugged stronghold of Cerro Prieta from which they continued to raid Spanish settlements. In 1753, the Seris offered to make peace with the Spanish if the white men would only return their women. But it was too late; the women were gone.

The Seris destroyed the Spanish mission at Guaymas and raided up and down the Sonoran frontier for another 20 years, emptying of residents the entire area between Hermosillo and Guaymas for fear of Seri wrath. By 1770, scarcity of food and weariness brought on by the extended state of siege caused the

Seri to disperse from Cerro Prieta. Many were rounded up and forced to live near Pitic. Those who didn't surrender lived on Tiburón and on the opposite coast along the Infernillo. In 1773, Father Chyrysotom founded the mission of Carrizal near the coast. Six months later, the mission was destroyed and the padre committed suicide. The former state of war again prevailed.

I made camp in the soft sands of the wash, stoking a tiny ironwood fire late into the night, watching Orion and the Hyades drift across the sky.

During the night a great horned owl decided to perch in a nearby dying palo verde tree. I pulled the wool stocking cap over my face hoping the night predator wouldn't mistake my nose for a bulbous deer mouse. Twenty minutes later I was close to sleep and the owl was still there. Unprovoked attacks of horned owls on humans were probably unknown. Still, just before I drifted off, I threw an arm across my face, further covering my nose.

A few hours before dawn, the intense longing of dreamtime startled me awake. Orion loomed on the western horizon. I missed my children.

Once again, I had left my family and other domestic responsibilities behind because these trips, the kind of revitalization they came to embody, were necessary beyond the daily onus of making a living. My wife knew this and generally approved of my expeditions. Like essential tribal forays, I had to have them. Abbey pioneered this sort of life and after four marriages had finally found a balance. Though it was the collective opinion of our friends that I was incapable of domestic living, I actually looked to Abbey for guidance in solving this central structural problem of my life: how to reconcile a life in the wild with love of home and family—a hope prefigured by the belief that one can live a fully human life despite the inevitable baggage of war.

Tiburón would be my last trip for a while, and probably the last while Ed was still walking the earth. Despite the costs, I was content to have come. Unlike our national parks or official wilderness areas, Tiburón had no trails or field and hiking guides facilitating easy travel. There were not even good topographical maps of the area. Exploration here necessitated both actual and metaphorical bushwhacking, the kind that stretched the mind. The plants were strange, and I didn't know what kinds of animals might live here. There could even have been wild Seris still hiding out in the barrancas of the Sierra Kunkaak. You came out here largely uninformed, with just an inkling of how to get around, and an even dimmer idea of what awaited you. It had always been my belief that the key to human evolution was the practice of hunting and, by going out to wild and unfamiliar places where dangerous animals also lived, I imagined myself honing my skills, cultivating the best qualities of the hunter: alertness, some courage, endurance, risk taking, solitude, patience, silence, and loyalty to the tribe.

Loyalty to the tribe was also the reason I had to leave this spirit-haunted desert island and return to Tucson. My nights on Tiburón had been visited by premonitions of some urgency: the jaguar dreams, for instance. I owed this loyalty to Ed, to our mutual friends and families, to his fans, to all the wilderness advocates and movements his books had spawned; I owed it to the clan. He had asked that I see to his burial, and I took the request seriously.

Ed Abbey had plans for his dying. He had a long time to think about it because the Western medical establishment had thoroughly fucked up his diagnosis and told him he had but six months to live five years before he actually died. During this time, he lived under the often-fluctuating certainty of a death sentence, and professional waffling as to whether anything might be done to modify the course of the disease—which probably was more important to me than to Ed. He carried this burden of misinformation with great dignity. I, however, with my usual animosity, deeply resented the medical profession's callous incompetence and cavalier stewardship of human life and carried this grudge all the way to Ed's grave.

Abbey was racing against the clock he knew was winding down fast, hurrying to flesh out his last work of fiction and a book of aphorisms before the end. He wanted to be buried simply, with dignity and some ceremony, in the desert by people who cared for him. Once I saw that he had entered his final days, this charge took precedence over everything else. It became a palpable trust every bit as solemn as lifeguarding a child or monkey wrenching a bulldozer.

Hidden among the logistics of death and burial were notions of duty that were tribal, based on respect, loyalty, and a shared belief in the value of wildness. This had more to do with Ed, who had thought these matters through, less with myself, who was merely carrying out the final wishes of an older, wiser brother. He had given me a mission. By the time of Tiburón, I no longer questioned this but simply signed on for the trip and rode out the consequences.

Sunrise. Waking to the descending notes of a canyon wren, I packed up and stashed my sleeping bag and heavier gear in a palo blanco tree, where it would be visible from surrounding hilltops when I tried to find it again on the way back. It was the day before we were to leave Tiburón. I was edgy and imagined receiving subliminal messages that not all was well at home: my marriage, Ed's health. I walked into the rising sun, weaving through small valleys and gentle hill country studded with columnar cactus and giant white-barked trees. A gray fox looked at me from a low saddle and slunk away. I reached the east coast of Tiburón sometime around mid-morning.

I climbed the summit of a little knoll populated by pitaya cactus and palo blanco trees, their long filament-like leaves reaching out from the stiff sea breeze blowing off the Infernillo. I listened to the rustle of those lovely trees and watched four buzzards cruise past the headlands. Frigate birds also soared overhead, and out above the strait an osprey made an abrupt dive, coming off with a sierra-sized fish. The Infernillo channel between the Sonoran mainland and Tiburón was shallow enough to see the tides moving in rills and rips, merging and crosscutting in a mosaic of brilliant reflections of the morning sun. I glassed the deeper water for whale spouts and looked for the heads of sea turtles. The Seris hunted several species of turtle, of which the giant leatherback sea turtle was the most important, an animal that figured centrally in both Seri diet and cosmology.

Overlooking the Infernillo, I tried to imagine the great migration of leatherback turtles that used to pass through, sea turtles floating in with the rising tides on mats of eel grass; below on the shallow dunes behind the beach, Seri men and woman emerging from the open shade under their ocotillo-branch ramadas to step into the scalding heat, ocean humidity boiling off the searing Sonoran coast in mid-July.

Here was the value of Tiburón: the land was a chunk of the original landscape from which we evolved, the homeland whose fragments today we regard as wilderness. You could still see the people, all people, and they were us, are us. It was also a place a renegade could regroup for another battle. I had been on a single plateau of life for so long it had come to feel much like a rut. Of growth I was clueless; a little change would do for now. Sitting on that hill on Tiburón, it occurred to me that I didn't want to go back to the old life.

The next morning the fisherman came. We loaded our gear into the panga and climbed in.

The island now loomed below a menacing sky. A stiff breeze skimmed brine off the tops of whitecaps and threw it in our faces. It looked like a storm was on the way.

We beached at Old Kino. I packed the equipment into my truck. On the way to Hermosillo we passed a knot of Seri women selling carvings and necklaces of tiny sea shells. I dropped my friends at the airport and headed north to Tucson.

2

ORIGINS

From Hermosillo, I blasted north along Mexican Highway Numero 15 in my not-so-environmentally-correct gas-guzzling Ford pickup at a cool 75 miles per hour, pausing once at the truck stop outside Benjamin Hill to fill up with Nova and wolf down a bowl of posole. I slowed in Santa Ana to look out the window at some elephants the traveling circus was watering in a vacant lot; nearby, along the late winter shade of a crumbling adobe wall, eight Bengal tigers twitched and wheeled inside cages mounted on the flatbed of a tractor trailer.

Just outside Magdalena, I felt a high-speed shimmy in the drivetrain. Leaning out the window, I heard the whine and rumble of something about to pop on the rear driveshaft. I pulled over and crawled under the pickup. The front universal joint was too hot to touch but I could tell by the play in the shaft it was getting ready to go. All the grease had burned off and the needle bearings were bone dry. The chance of getting a "U" joint that would work in Magdalena was not good, and I didn't have time to transplant one from the front driveshaft or to mess around with a busted-down vehicle. I could try to baby the truck back to Tucson or abandon the son of a bitch and hitch a ride to Nogales where I could have someone come pick me up. If I left the pickup in Mexico, the odds of returning a week later to a burned-out, engine-less, steel hulk propped up on blocks were excellent. But I had to get back; I was thinking about Abbey.

I squirted 40-weight motor oil on the joint, lubricating the sucker as best I could. I nursed the truck northward toward Magdalena, listening obsessively, an ancient habit acquired from a lifetime of driving beat-up old rigs that threatened to break down at any time and whose potential malfunction dominated every moment of driving.

In Magdalena I had the universal joint packed with lubricant. I took a cup of chassis grease with me, stowed in a Tecate can with the top cut off. I pulled over every 30 miles to repack the bearings.

I emptied my mind and let the countryside seep back in. A number of serious questions about my relationship with Ed Abbey remained unanswered. Time was too short to deal with most of them. What is the true path of friendship when the friend is dying or dead? Should I simply wish him to get better? If Ed were a much younger friend my "duty" might be just to try to keep him alive or make his last days as full and comfortable as possible. But this was not the case. Ed would not accept living outside the organic circle of life. There was a time to live and a time to die.

The greatest gift I could give my friend might be simply to honor his wishes into death and beyond. How many friends would risk jail and big fines to illegally dispose of a dead comrade? I grinned. That was my value to Abbey: the recklessness of Hayduke.

Past Imuris, on the warm south-facing cliffs, yellow brittlebush blossomed. A fine crop of green grass and filaree sprouted under the shade of mesquite trees and scrubs. A few yellow Mexican poppies speckled the roadside. The big trees in the riparian bottoms had begun to bud and green up, the muted gray-green of young sycamore leaves and deeper green of the early cottonwoods. Spring might be coming early.

This lush land, the topography and vegetation largely unchanged for centuries, on the border of territories once occupied by Pima, Opata, Seri, and Apache Indians, still carried a grace of old Mexico that eluded the American retirement communities and artsy-fartsy towns of Green Valley or Tubac just north of the border. You could travel along the Rio Bambuto, the dark ribbon of permanent flowing water undiminished by industrial pumping and large-scale irrigation; walk the coarse cobbles washed out of the foothills of the Sierra Madre, under the canopy of early spring foliage—the cottonwood, sycamore, live oak, canyon ash, hackberry, and black walnut trees just beginning to leaf out—and imagine the richness of life that was here until very recently: the great Sonoran megafauna, the Mexican wolf, jaguar, wild turkey, Sonoran pronghorn, mountain lion, bighorn sheep, mule and white-tailed deer, peccary and grizzly bear, animals that lingered here into the present century and, except for the grizzly and maybe the lobo, still roamed the more remote pockets of this land; all these wild creatures living for millennia with native peoples, later with the Spanish, Mexicans, and ourselves for a brief moment of history. Then you could wander eastward into the foothills, where wolves and jaguars still prowl, up-and-down country with forests of giant pitaya cactus growing on the lower slopes, the Sierra Pinito and southeast to the valley of the Rio Bacanuchi, grasslands now, into the zone of oak and agave, up and through the range of cedar and two-needle pine, beyond into the three-needle ponderosa, called Apache or Chihuahua pine here, where giant woodpeckers and strange parrot-like birds live among fir and even a rare spruce at the headwaters of the Rio Yaqui, empty country where grizzlies are rumored to live, finally arriving on the wild and rugged divide of the Sierra Madre, a place you thought could only exist in legend.

That place was the northern range of Tarahumara Indian country, now abandoned and largely without people, the edge of the great barranca country. Abbey had been down there once, and I had been planning a trip myself for over a decade.

I like to think this way about the country as I drive through it. It helps me appreciate the land if I imagine myself a hunter-gatherer trying to reside in it. What I mean is that this pretty hill country with its clean washes, diverse flora, and abundant animal community is a good place to live. Only our imagination has abandoned such places. And I could take up residency here again if I had to; such rich and easy country, well watered yet mild of climate, neither blistering in summer nor frigid in winter, with plenty of game, caves for shelter, and good oak firewood.

Just south of Nogales, a single-engine aircraft was taking off, probably a Cessna 185. Both Abbey and I had flown out of this same little airstrip on such a plane, a milestone in our friendship as it marked a rapprochement. Back in February of 1977, famed desert bush pilot Ike Russell had flown Ed and me, along with three other friends, to an improvised airstrip hacked out of the brittlebush and bursage (on which only Ike had landed) on the uninhabited island of Angel de la Guarda far out in the Sea of Cortez, fifteen kilometers off the Baja Coast. When Ike returned to the island five days later to pick up Ed and the three friends, he left me behind for ten additional days on Isla Angel. For me, it was like getting thrown into the briar patch: to be abandoned on a desert island, forced to camp alone by the sea—the essence of everything I loved best about Baja and gulf islands, that marriage of ocean and cactus. In short, a dream come true. This period of solitude also came at a time when I badly needed it. Nothing serious, just the usual mid-thirties metaphysical doldrums, when indecision ruled: what to do, whom to be, where to go, whether to go on. The gas and Ike's expenses, along with my ten days of solitude, were Ed's present to me on the eve of a long period of quarreling over the *The Monkey Wrench Gang*, the publication and popularity of which had generated mutual ambivalence between Ed and me concerning our personal gifts and debts to each other, in short, for the naked respect in which we each held for the undiluted value of the other's character.

Reflecting on our desert trip, I remembered the first time I ran into Ed. It was after the war, after the other metamorphosis.

^^^

It was 1968. I felt my life had been consumed; the flames of the war in Southeast Asia had incinerated the remains of my middle-American existence and from the ashes had arisen the Peacock-bird, more reduced than renewed, that Ed Abbey first met. My life before Vietnam, my previous existence as a boy growing up in Michigan, a student activist, had ended during Tet in 1968.

The biographical skeleton of my life was as familiar as ragweed: I grew up in Michigan with a loving family and an unremarkable childhood. I did spend considerable time in the woods. I suffered the average adolescence but read a lot of books. As a teenager, I discovered the Rocky Mountains and deserts of the Southwest. I hated college and left the Midwest to pound nails and work in copper mines in the American West. The military eventually caught up with me. I volunteered for the draft but chafed under military command and a partial accommodation to this mismatch led me to become a Green Beret medic and to go to Vietnam.

In my life, Vietnam and the wilderness landscapes of the American West remain welded. At the exact same time Ed Abbey was making his first foray into the Cabeza Prieta desert of southwestern Arizona (the place where the two of us would take our last walk) during February of 1968, I survived the Tet Offensive in the relative security of a hospital in the former Republic of South Vietnam, where I was interned with 30 unfortunate marines whose wounds were not sufficiently dire to get them medevaced back to Japan or Stateside. I spent my brief convalescence in the Danang Naval Hospital with the other grunts lying under our bunks listening to the war—mortar and rocket rounds exploding everywhere, gun ships screaming overhead, my fingers clutching an illegal .45 automatic, the only defensive weapon on the ward against the platoon of North Vietnamese sappers who were blasting through the perimeter wire only 50 meters away—but still knowing I was infinitely better off than my Green Beret strikeforce teammates, who at that same moment were being cut to ribbons and rolled over by NVA tanks at Lang Vei near Khe Sanh.

Five days after Tet, I went AWOL from the hospital and returned to the team at an A-camp at Bato, deep in enemy country in the Central Highlands of Quang Ngai Province. The Tet offensive in the countryside lagged a couple of weeks behind the fighting in the cities, but it did come and with a vengeance. Hundreds of civilians were displaced and killed (and were later added to the body count and reported by American Command as "enemy KIA"). As senior medic on the Bato A-team, I pieced together Montagnard children who had been caught in the crossfire until I began to lose my mind. Standing in the monsoon rain, holding a dead, gunshot baby, I cursed God.

I arranged to leave Vietnam at that moment, in the middle of my second tour, as my Army enlistment was about to expire. The day I packed my bags for home, March 16, 1968, American soldiers ruthlessly murdered at least 508 Vietnamese civilians 40 miles north of us, in a place called My Lai.

Home from the war zone, back in the World as we called it, it was early spring of 1968. I bought a jeep in Michigan and drove west, hoping to look up my two oldest friends from the Midwest. One worked as a teacher on the Navajo Reservation. We had been together at the University of Michigan where I had been associated with civil rights politics and the beginnings of the New Left. As an independent student activist, I had invited and brought Martin Luther King Jr. to the campus to speak. Two weeks after leaving Vietnam and a day after joining my friend in Fort Defiance, Arizona, King was assassinated. My response to the murder bothered my old friend a great deal: I was not surprised that someone had finally got to him. I had known that Dr. King had powerful enemies and, in 1968, this was what I expected of the world. By the time summer rolled around and Bobby Kennedy was killed, I was convinced the world had gone quite mad, and I retreated into the wilderness to deal with it.

The other friend lived in Colorado. This ex-roommate was an intellectual, a baseball nut, a music lover, and a city dweller whom I greatly admired but had never known as an outdoorsman. But, by late 1968, my friend was a big Sierra Club guy, a dedicated environmentalist, serious backpacker and mountain climber. The reason for these changes was a man named Edward Abbey. Earlier that year, he had published a book called *Desert Solitaire.* This book changed lives.

I had walked out of Vietnam with a bottomless weariness of war and an empty tank. Within the year, I ran into Ed. It was probably no accident. Though I didn't realize it for many years, that nasty little Asian war opened the door to our 20-year friendship: it was the valence that bound wildness, Hayduke, Peacock, Abbey, and the battle for wilderness into the same soup.

Vietnam was the crucible that forged my own militancy, identifying for me my real enemies and the real war, the one being waged against life on earth. The reality of the political lies I witnessed during the Tet Offensive was confirmed a year later by release of photos of the My Lai massacre: on that day, ex-Sergeant E-5 D. A. Peacock was forever shut of home.

And, at 27 years of age, I believed that I had at least glimpsed what the civilized world had to offer and knew then I would not trade a single day in the wilderness for a lifetime of such riches. By late 1968, I was ready for something as demanding and dangerous as war but aimed in the direction of life. My values were somehow intact but the killing had drained all else out. Wounded but dedicated, I was a committed whacko, a fanatic willing to go the distance at any drop of the hat, a warrior who didn't believe in killing strangers. I was looking for a war worth fighting.

Abbey had already identified his own battleground: the wilderness of the American West. Not too long after the two of us met, he noticed my talents—my useful training and that great anger going to waste—and determined how it might be used.

That meeting took place in Tucson. Bill Eastlake, a mutual friend, called me up and told me to come on over. In 1969 William Eastlake was the grand old man of Southwestern letters, and so remained, despite the poisonous seasonality of New York publishing. I hopped on my motorcycle and drove up and down the desert roads at the foot of the Santa Catalina Mountains until I located Eastlake's house that, back then, was beyond the edge of the giant cow-plop that had become Tucson. Some people were there, possibly writer-types, but I didn't know them. The winter air had chilled me and my hands shook as I pulled out a baggy of Bugler tobacco and rolled a joint-like cigarette. The cold palsied my fingers and I had trouble striking a match. The man sitting next to me gave me a light. He was a tall rangy man with a short dark beard. We talked about mountain lions, a subject he was up on because he had just written a piece for *LIFE Magazine.* He worked as a seasonal ranger at Organ Pipe Cactus National Monument in southwestern Arizona and his name was Ed Abbey. He invited me to visit.

A week later I threw my sleeping bag in my jeep and drove down to Organ Pipe bearing gifts: a six pack of beer and a bottle of whiskey. That was how you visited people in those days. (Abbey had first visited William Eastlake in Cuba, New Mexico, nervously knocking at Bill's door with bottle of gin in hand.) I met up with Ed after work in the government Quonset hut he shared with Bill Hoy and other rangers south of Ajo. From a nearby room, someone nostalgically played Grofe's Grand Canyon Suite, and Ed noted he was taking a lookout job on the North Rim, one of the four corners of his desert world, staking out the territory that the big gulch held in his heart. We drank and talked until early in the morning, late for a working man. I was new to that part of the country, and Ed directed me to Dripping Springs, one of two natural, permanent water sources in Organ Pipe. The late winter morning was warm and yellow blossoms of brittlebush foretold the approaching spring. I hiked a short trail to a small cave. Within the grotto lay a milky pool, pale and oracular, draining into a brushy draw swarming with honey bees. I retreated along the well-used foot trail, hard-packed by the boots of hundreds of visitors.

Later, less than a mile away but still in Organ Pipe, I found mountain lion tracks in a sand wash. Abbey had told me that Organ Pipe, though lush and captivating in desert terms, was relatively tame compared to the great expanse of land adjacent to the west and northwest, the wild and empty valleys and ranges of the Cabeza Prieta, the great desert wilderness that would be his final resting site.

You can't rebuild a life that has no structure to begin with. In 1969, I was still reeling from a year and a half of Vietnam. I had no desire to "re-enter society" nor any talent for reform. The precise problem seemed to be that I wanted a life but not the world "they" said I'd have to live it in. Though estranged from my own time and without a clue as to how to proceed, I was not lost; I knew that my real homeland, the one I would fight the authentic war over, the one I would die for, was out in the deserts and mountains. This man Abbey had a distant but deep passion, a humorous fanaticism about defending the wild I found attractive.

That next summer, derangement surfaced again and I considered returning to Vietnam. I don't know quite why because by then it seemed clear that I couldn't change anything, that if a person really wanted the war to end, he'd fight for peace on the streets here. But I was a loner and dreams of Vietnam haunted me. If I could just get over there one more time, I told myself, I might make a difference; at least, I'd share the danger and the suffering: the veteran's not uncommon delusion of revisiting the specific horror and changing it, getting it right this time. So, I entertained the notion of going back to Southeast Asia as a photojournalist. I scored a graduate fellowship in Intensive Vietnamese, a language I already knew, and traveled to the University of Hawaii to snorkel and watch fish for three months, during which I studied more Vietnamese. While I was there I heard Ed Abbey's wife had died of leukemia, so I wrote him a note saying though I didn't know him very well, I was thinking about him.

Some time went by and he wrote back wondering if I wanted to take a trip into the canyon country. I returned home and decided to take Ed up on a visit to the southern Utah wilderness.

A month later, I picked Ed up in Kanab, Utah, just north of the Grand Canyon. We drove east along the Vermillion Cliffs, turned north on a dirt road tracing a bench above the Paria and on into Cottonwood Canyon. We bounced on toward Kodachrome Basin with the dark spine of the Kaiparowits Plateau lying in the gray distance. I had seen southern Utah before but not much of it, and never anything like this: feminine landscapes of bentonite, soft clay hills with lenses of blue and green, badlands disappearing under the coarse angular red scree from the cliffs above, the massive faces of windblown Navajo and Wingate sandstone, their dark patina stained and decorated by seeps and runoff.

South of Kodachrome Basin, amid a wasteland of rabbitbrush and juniper, we pulled off the rutted road to an old drill-rig site. The rig was gone and the hole was capped, but part of the frame remained along with sections of pipe and used bits; the spot site was deserted but not abandoned. The drilling outfit was coming back, probably to look for coal deposits to fuel a proposed coal-burning power plant at Kaiparowits forty miles to the north. Ed found a spanner and fit the big wrench around the cap and removed it. We dropped in a rock, then pieces of pipe and chain to see how deep the hole was: nothing, only wind sounds whistling down the casing. Ed found some more junk lying around, and I located a pile of used-up diamond drill bits. All this went down the hole.

"Should take them a while to drill through all that junk," said Abbey. Then he grinned. "Someone has to do it."

We passed through the little town of Escalante, then turned back south on the sandstone rimrock. We paused at Dance Rock, where Mormon pioneers stopped their wagons to hold a dance in 1879. These men, women, children, and babies, under orders from Brigham Young, left their homes in south-central Utah to establish a new settlement at Bluff, near Four Corners. The settlers had to lower their wagons and livestock down into Glen Canyon, then up the other side, and on to 1500-foot-high Comb's Ridge, finally blasting through with hammers and drills.

"Those old Mormons were tough," noted Abbey, even-handed in his credits.

We crept southward over the rock toward the heads of Hurricane, Coyote, and Davis gulches. Soon, we parked our rig, scouted the rimrock for routes, then shouldered our packs and edged down a wash that quickly grew into a canyon. Logs of agatized fossil wood, washed down from the Kaiparowits, littered the upper wash, and some of the logs were a couple of feet across, the annular rings now silicified into lovely red and yellow agate used by the Anasazi to chip arrowheads. The canyon sank into the slickrock, a deep, narrow slot with a ribbon of sky above. Off to the right lay an alcove under the stain of waterfall that coursed in from the rim during the rains. On one side a horned anthropomorph shape was carved into the rock between two smaller figures with wide shoulders and tapered bodies. We broke for food and Ed heated up a can of chili by propping the can between two suitable rocks then igniting twigs, one at a time, under the can. I was impressed with his skill and this stark efficiency in contrast to my own style of wilderness bonfires.

Late in the afternoon, we turned up a short box canyon. A creek trickled out and in the damp sand were tracks of deer and coyotes. We moved upstream above the range of cattle, passing three small beaver dams of willow. Just as the last sunlight filtered down into the canyon, we came to the dead end. The sheer cliffs closed in on three sides and at the bottom of the box canyon was a plunge pool of striking beauty—clear water surrounded by cottonwood and canyon ash—an Asian scene of dappled light and stark dendrite shadows cast against the red rock cliffs.

The next morning we hiked down the main canyon until the creek turned sluggish then disappeared under the rising waters of Lake Powell, the man-made outrage visible from space, which had drowned the loveliest of all canyons: Glen Canyon. For Ed, who had been fortunate enough to float through Glen Canyon, this dam symbolized everything evil in our industrial culture.

With a floating willow stick, I scratched an obscenity against the Bureau of Reclamation in the mud. Ed sat silently on a rock. As we turned to go, Ed asked me if I knew anything about explosives. I replied that I had been field cross-trained in simple demolitions as a Green Beret and had filled in for our wounded demolition sergeant in Quang Ngai Province during the summer of 1967.

Two days later we hiked out and sat out a thunderstorm in the International Scout I had borrowed from a girlfriend in Tucson. After four dry days of backpacking fare we wanted drink and real food. I found some beer and a chocolate bar; Ed came up with some cheese and a bottle of bourbon. After several permutations, we decided that beer, cheese, and crackers were the best complement, followed by an after-dinner drink of whiskey and snack of chocolate. I had a cheap little tape player, and I slipped in a late quartet of Beethoven, the Fifteenth. Thunder crashed and sheets of rain ran down the windshield; beyond, through the mist, lay a ghostly wasteland of dull-red and golden slickrock, fossilized hummocks of sand dune, dotted here and there with a bush of cliff rose or a juniper tree.

Later, I would look back to this time and wonder what the hell it was we saw in one another. Ed was older than I so there was that edge to our friendship. He seemed more sullen and grouchy than charismatic to me. And, 20 years ago, I was hardly a prize; I only smiled when drinking beer and the slightest sudden movement, noise, or trauma would bring out what I called "the cornered-ferret aspect" of my otherwise charming personality. Ed was actually tolerant of this erratic conduct, believing it a fated and necessary part of the "determined crazy" category of whacko Vietnam Vet behavior.

On the other hand, I had read *Desert Solitaire* and could see that a big chunk of the modern conservation movement had its origins right here. I could understand why a land ethic grew out of this southern Utah slickrock and why its protectors tended to be so militant. *Desert Solitaire* was something larger than just a book about the desert. It was about the power of the land, of human connections to the earth, an idea of freedom. Ed's book was a call to arms.

Of course, we all had to make a living. After our Escalante hike, Ed got a fire lookout job on the North Rim of Grand Canyon to supplement his earnings as a writer. I moved into a place outside Tucson and took a temporary job as a mailman. When the job ended, Ed Abbey, heartbroken after getting dumped by his girlfriend, came down and camped out in my backyard. Ed found a stone house near Sabino Canyon. I quit my mailman job and chased a girl to Cape Cod. Ed lived in the stone house and worked as a writer. I came back and moved into the stone house with him, then flitted off again for northern California following another woman. Ed took up with my old friend, the woman who had lent me the International Scout on our Escalante trip; she moved in with him for a bit. The three of us went camping in the Cabeza Prieta. Ed and I took backpacking trips into the Superstition Mountains, the Dripping Springs Mountains, the Gilas, and the Galiuros. We did several more truck-camping trips into the Cabeza Prieta. Abbey got the two of us a job working for the Defenders of Wildlife as "custodians" of a large, private wildlife refuge in Aravaipa Canyon. We split the job since both of us wanted at least six months to travel. Actually, it was more a non-job since there was nothing to do but live there. We explored the country and, in November of 1972, I caught a glimpse of the last

Arizona wild lobo, a Mexican wolf with a considerable reputation as an expert ham stringer of calves. In the end, however, we both found the country tame; we wanted freedom. I lasted a few more months; Ed hung on for nearly a year. We were restless.

That winter we started taking out billboards and bulldozers, and plotting against strip mines, dams, copper smelters, and logging operations. The "Monkey Wrench Days" had begun, though I was unaware of any larger context for our mischief. As a team, we were careless and ineffective, almost recreational in our sloth, abstract in our political theory. It was simply something to do; a raised fist against the blind greed of technology, an anodyne to impotence. The driving force in our misbehavior was probably an idea Ed had for a book he'd just started to write.

Ed Abbey gave me another gift that year: job advice. Though essentially unemployable, I too had bills to pay. Ed advised applying for seasonal work with the National Park Service.

"Douglas, they give you a quitting date to look forward to."

I got out the atlas and put in applications for all the places I might want to visit during the summer months, including a new park in Washington State, North Cascades National Park. I was offered a job as a Backcountry Ranger, a good job because you lived out of your backpack and slept out under the stars or in a tent every night. I climbed mountains, crossed glaciers, explored remote alpine basins, and got paid for it. The job lasted until late summer, 1975. But as a ranger, a lawman of the federal government, I was a dismal failure, citing only an illegally parked Winnebago after three years of police work. Anarchists tend to make poor law enforcement agents. Eventually, having fallen from Interior Department grace by wrecking a government pickup and by engaging in an altercation with a Watcom County deputy sheriff, I would leave for a fire lookout job in Glacier National Park, Montana, to the immense relief of the staff of North Cascades. Before leaving Washington State, however, I would take up the plight of grizzly bears, meet a woman I would marry, and eventually receive a new book from Edward Abbey cryptically autographed:

"To Douglas who is of course the hero of this here book."

I had known about the book Ed was writing. Abbey told me about it on New Year's Day of 1974—the day we came up with the idea of a trip to Tiburón Island. We were camped out in the Sierra Pinta Range on the Cabeza Prieta down near the Mexican border in southwestern Arizona. No one lived there and very few adventurers traveled the unmaintained jeep trails into this most stark of desert landscapes.

Abbey and I had driven my pickup west from Tucson through the Growler Range into the Cabeza Prieta Wildlife Refuge, then blasted up the coalescing alluvial fans of the valley bottom, the bajada, north around the Granite Range. It was then late December and we were now within the boundary of the military bombing and gunnery range. We kept going until after dark, making camp for the night under a giant ironwood tree. The next morning we moved out early to avoid the Air Force jets. We drove through Montrose Well west into the Mohawk Valley. At the low pass we found bighorn sheep tracks, always a big deal since desert bighorn were rare. Just east of Sunday Pass, the white rumps and tails of four pronghorn flagged us above the sea of creosote as the antelope bounced away toward a big gap between rugged peaks in the Bryan Mountains, the wave of bajada sweeping up and over and into the next valley, through the fangs of protruding granite buried to the shoulder in their own detritus.

Later, on New Year's Eve at Eagle Tank, at the foot of the eastern escarpment of the Sierra Pinta, it sleeted and snowed on us, an unusual occurrence. We sat out the rain for a day under a tarp, stoking an ironwood fire. We charted the desert islands we wanted to visit in the Sea of Cortez, Isla Tiburón, and Angel de la Guarda. Ed scribbled notes on the book he had been writing for the past couple years, *The Monkey Wrench Gang.*

By the next morning the sky had cleared and it was chilly by desert standards. We decided to hike north along the base of the Sierra Pinta to Sunday Pass, through which possibly no one had passed in a decade. The country was that big, that unused. Nonetheless, we were out here on the edge of the "Bombing Range" and had neglected to obtain an official "Hold harmless" permit. As part of his research on the *Monkey Wrench* book, Abbey had purchased a lot of Army surplus gear including a huge camouflage net, which we stretched over my pickup to hide it from whatever military aircraft might be in the area.

We walked north on game trails at the foot of the truncated slabs of uplifted granite. The tracks of mule deer, jackrabbits, and bighorn sheep traced the faint pathway. A few potsherds attested to much older usage by prehistoric Indians. Ed wanted to explore a steep, short canyon. The two of us climbed up a slot, a dry waterfall that ran only during torrential summer rains. The dark lichen streak where the water ran was slippery so we "chimney-ed" up the coarser pegmatitic rock on the side until we reached a tiny plunge pool thirty or forty feet up. A few gallons of precious rainwater filled the basin. It would dry up within two months if it didn't rain again. Sometimes you went six months out here with no rain. Both Ed and I marked the location of the tiny tinaja on our topographic maps for future reference; we wanted to walk across the Cabeza someday.

At the foot of Sunday Pass an ancient sheep skull lay on the desert pavement. The bighorn's corrugated horns looked like they were unraveling with age.

"The Indians probably ambushed it from the rocks," Ed observed. I said there used to be a pile of bighorn sheep skulls just across the pass at Heart Tank.

"I always wanted to go there," said Ed, "maybe I'll make it before I die."

"It's incredibly beautiful," I said, "and always full of water."

"Must have been a great place to live," noted Abbey, "spearing sheep by moonlight, living under an ocotillo ramada, making love in the sunlight. . . ."

Just then we both looked up. From far across the valley we could hear the deep *thunk-thunk-thunk* of chopper blades. I raised my binoculars and glassed the southeast; about a mile away an olive-drab Chinook helicopter was skimming the desert bajada and coming right at us. Probably just a routine military patrol but we didn't feel like doing any explaining about being out here with no permit. Ed and I instinctively jumped down off the boulder-strewn pass into the sand wash below. The only vegetation high enough to hide a man grew there. We hit the dirt under a big palo verde tree and hid our faces, careful not to look up. The chopper roared overhead, then disappeared over the pass.

Both of us breathing heavily, Ed looked at me.

"You're shaking, Douglas." He put his hand on my shoulder.

"I guess I still take this shit seriously," I muttered, "those fuckers out here buzzing the wilderness just like when the helicopter used to hose down on me in Vietnam."

"What helicopter was that?" Ed asked.

"It was just one of our choppers, you know, those flyboys up there don't care who they hose down on. It's just something to shoot at. Water buffalo, Montagnard babies, Green Beret medics, all the same to them. Every time I see one of the fuckers I get the same feeling, waiting once again for that drilling sensation of machine-gun bullets ventilating me."

I stood up and brushed the sand off my clothes. I was still trembling. The sky was clouding up again. I shook my head and turned to Ed.

"I think for me helicopters are evil incarnate. In Nam they dealt indiscriminate death from the sky while answering to no one. Every time I see a chopper, I imagine a ball of fire. I think I'd like to shoot the fucker down. Especially here. The worst place, the place I hate the most to see a hovering helicopter with their death technology is in the wilderness. I'd never kill a stranger again but I'd die to protect a wild place."

"So would I," said Edward Abbey.

We made it back to camp by late afternoon. The unusual wet weather settled back in. It began to drizzle. I got a fire going. We moved our camp chairs close to the blaze. We opened beers. I had recovered some from the shock of the low-lying chopper but was still a bit shaky. Ed had been very kind and supportive. This was the soul of the man I grew to love. Edward Abbey possessed a prodigious intelligence and he could be quite intimidating. But not today. Ed had been exceedingly gentle during what I would later identify as "one of my flashbacks." I asked him more about his idea for the book, about the book's theme, "No Compromise in Defense of the Wilderness," and what it was he really cared about.

"People," he said, "people like you and our friends and families. I would never sell out a friend for an idea. A single brave deed is worth a hundred books and this book will be no different."

Huddled around a soggy desert campfire in 1974, we drank a toast of beer. Above the granitic spires, soaring below the rare roof of heavy desert clouds, a big dark bird emerged then faded into the gloom. We toasted the golden eagle of Eagle Tank, as uncommon as the Arizona sleet and scudding clouds. We popped another beer and drank to friends, wilderness, our upcoming trip to Tiburón Island, and the success of Ed's mission and his new novel.

3
LAST DAYS

I passed through customs without incident. The Border Patrol in Nogales could be real swine, though they occasionally surprised you with good humor and competence. This time they confiscated a cache of five illegal limes. I moved on, looking out the window at Johnny's Cafe before I turned on I-19 north. Five miles north I caught myself staring again, this time at the Molina family restaurant at Pete Kitchen's old ranch, as renowned for their sun-dried machaca—shredded grass-fed beef dried with onion, garlic, and chilies—as Johnny's Cafe was for good menudo made from cooking prime honeycombed tripe with hominy and six baby pig's feet for five hours. I was hungry.

But there was no time for food. Ed might be dying. He could be dead. I could have called to find out, though phones were beside the point. My job was burial.

North of Tucson, I turned west across the Santa Cruz River, a stream that used to flow year-round from Nogales through Tucson and on toward the Gila, a fertile ribbon formerly visited by grizzlies ranging down from the Santa Rita Mountains. I passed the Mosaic Cafe, another reliable source of menudo and carne seca. I still wanted something to eat. Maybe tonight, if Ed wasn't dead, if he felt up to it, I'd grill some game birds over mesquite, basting them with olive oil, lime juice, garlic, and cilantro, washing them down with a couple bottles of Pinot Grigio. I pulled in to Ed's yard.

There he was, still alive, though pallid with anemia, white as a sheet. He'd had another bout of esophageal bleeding. I tried to tell Ed about the Tiburón trip and talk to him about a rancher we both knew of who was killing mountain lions, but he wasn't listening.

"Douglas," he said, "where the hell is that .357 Magnum pistol?"

Those were the last days of February 1989. The outer world was preoccupied with the usual truck of commerce, the 17th running of Iditarod, the death sentence of writer Salman Rushdie for satire and blasphemy, for the kind of writing Abbey did. Not much was happening on the environmental scene. Earth First!, the radical environmental group much inspired by *The Monkey Wrench Gang*, was reportedly under investigation by the FBI.

A few days later, on March 4th, Ed made a last public appearance, a benefit reading for Earth First! at the El Rio Community Center in Tucson. After a pep rally spearheaded by Dave Foreman, Kat Clarke, actually an undercover FBI agent who had maneuvered herself into the Master of Ceremony job, introduced Ed.

I arrived late and stood in the wings. Five-year-old Becky Abbey was there and I picked her up on my shoulders so she could see her father. Ed's choice for the reading was a chapter from his unfinished manuscript, *Hayduke Lives*, a chapter called "Earth First! Rendezvous," which was an account of a real Earth First! rendezvous that had taken place in 1988 up on the North Rim of Grand Canyon and was also infiltrated by the FBI.

It turned out the FBI was well represented at that last appearance in Tucson. Had I not been preoccupied with Abbey's failing health, his daughter, and our quarrel, I might have been able to spot undercover FBI Special Agent Michael Fain, who buddied up to me and later bought me several beers. All the time, an FBI helicopter circled overhead to record our conversation, which I was to learn about two months later.

Abbey finished. Applause. I remember having the distinct feeling that the audience had unknowingly shared the honor of both a private and a historic moment because there wouldn't be another Ed Abbey reading. Ed turned to leave, caught my eye, and walked straight over to me. He bent down, eyes flashing, and spit a demand in my ear: "Douglas, get me that fucking pistol back. I need it."

The last ten days of Abbey's life lingers yet as a haze of rage and recrimination. We weren't listening to each other until just before the end; he was fixed on the .357 and I was preoccupied with mountain lions. Ed was angry because I wouldn't come up with the Magnum pistol, and he kept demanding I get it for him.

I kept putting him off and he was furious. Accusations went back and forth. Though other pistols lay on the shelf, he wanted the Ruger. I knew what for and maybe I owed him that option.

My own rage had to do with cougars. The picture that got my attention was a grainy black-and-white blow up: a photograph of a pyramid of mountain lion heads, seventeen of them I think, although the picture was cropped and you could only see the full face of fifteen. Cut off more or less at the neck, stacked one on top of another at the base of a tree or stump, the larger ones were at the bottom of the pile, some fanged and gaped-mouth, others clinched-jawed, all with eyes closed in death, surprisingly fresh-looking, as if they had all been recently killed.

Though obsessed with dead cats and feuding constantly with Ed about the pistol, I was nonetheless aware that he was slowly bleeding to death. As it turned out, it wasn't all that slow. I wanted him somehow to pull through, as he had before. But he had his own agenda, and I think he had decided that this was the time to go.

Little things betrayed this finality, things he said or talked about, such as his physical weakness due to blood loss, his inability to hike out into the Cabeza Prieta. Or—out of the blue—about the desire for immortality and how it is based on a terrible fear of death, which comes from having not lived fully, from a cowardly, tedious, and uneventful life, and how the worst thing of all would be to cling to this kind of life using the medical technology of life-support systems. "If your life has been wasted, then naturally you're going to cling like a drowning man to whatever kind of semi-life medical technology can offer you, and you're going to end up in a hospital with a dozen tubes sticking in your body, machines keeping your organs going. Which is the worst possible way to die. One's death should mean something. Those who fear death most are those who enjoy life least. Death is every man's final critic," Ed said. "To die well you must live bravely."

Of course, we all knew what Ed had in mind for his funeral. He was well prepared for this last trip as the medical doctors gave him plenty of advance notice, having misdiagnosed his condition as cancer of the pancreas, telling him he was in danger of immediate death for a half decade. So Ed left written instructions.

> Funeral Instructions—Body to be transported in bed of pickup truck and to be buried as soon as possible in a hole dug on our private property up in La Sal's or at Cliff Dwellers. No undertakers wanted; no embalming (for godsake!); no coffin. Just a plain pine box hammered together by a friend; or an old sleeping bag, or tarp, will do. If site selected is too rocky for burial, then pile on sand and a pile of stones sufficient to keep coyotes from dismembering and scattering my bones. Wrap body in my anarchist flag. But bury if possible; I want my body to help fertilize the growth of a cactus, or cliffrose, or sagebrush, or tree, etc.

I thought I knew Ed well enough to believe that what was important here was entering the Round River of Life. The selection of the site would be a matter of practical discretion, taste, and sensibility. On the other hand, he was dead serious about burial, about the coyotes not getting it all: Ed wanted to nourish a community of plants.

Still, we squabbled over the gun.

"When are you going to get that goddamn .357 back here?"

"You cantankerous sonofabitch," I struck back; "you just can't wait to die, can you? Well, fuck you."

I went home, deeply troubled this time, and wrote Ed a letter, the first serious one in a decade, about our children, explaining why I couldn't let him have the gun. He never got to read the letter, though it's buried with him.

I drove the letter over to Ed's house. Clarke came running down the driveway. She had been calling me; Ed was hemorrhaging. We set off for the hospital. I was in the lead car, an old

Honda, taking Clarke down the middle of Grant Road, lights flashing, horn honking. Ed was behind in Dave Foreman's car, with Dave's wife, Nancy, a nurse, administering to him. A chubby young blond in a red corvette tried to cut me off just to be smart. She didn't know this was a life-and-death run, of course. She was in the lane to my right, alongside me. A power pole was coming up at the next corner. I swerved into her and tried to drive her into the pole. Just like that, just to get rid of her and get the job done. Her quick reflexes and fast car saved her. Madness.

At the hospital, Ed submitted—for the sake of the people he loved—to the high-tech medicine he hated. There, I tried to persuade him, using all of my talents, to undergo things that might have saved his life. I talked him into an operation to relieve the source of local high blood pressure. I felt a surge of guilt, then remembered we were in this together and that I was not merely executing his last wishes. I put myself in his place and told the truth. Try it for the children, I argued, it'll only mean another day in the fucking hospital. What do you have to lose?

The portal shunt worked, though it was late in the course of his bleeding to death. Had this operation been done months before, Abbey might still be alive.

During the two days and nights in the medical facility, Clarke Abbey, Jack Loeffler, and I waited and watched. We struggled with the hope that modern medicine might produce miracles, counterbalanced by our promise not to let him die in the hospital. Ed's two grown sons flew in. We needed our own doctor; Clarke's brother-in-law, Steve Prescott, a Salt Lake City M.D., joined us. The medical data were analyzed. All Ed needed to live another decade or two was to not bleed anymore and to get a blood transfusion. But Ed wouldn't go for more technical intervention. This was it.

If there remained any question about Abbey's life, it was answered by his dying. Despite the indignities and bodily invasions he suffered, he forgave and never wavered.

I had been experiencing strongly ambivalent emotions because I now thought it was possible for Abbey to live out a more or less normal life if he could just survive this current episode. But, why was I pushing so hard for him to live if he had decided it was time to move on? More important, a deal had been struck; we had promised Ed he wouldn't have to die in the hospital. Finally, he pulled out all the tubes and announced, with the clearest eyes I had ever seen, that it was time to go.

Steve, who seemed the most level-headed of our tiny group, reminded me of our bargain and we quickly packed up Ed's room. Clarke said, "Doug, you pick the spot [for Ed to die] and lead the way." Jack backed up his pickup to the door of the Intensive Care Ward. I told Clarke it would take about 40 minutes to get there.

I shook hands with the two duty nurses and thanked them. We loaded Ed into the front seat of Jack's truck, propped him up between Clarke and Jack, and headed east on Grant Road, toward the Tucson Mountains. At the railroad tracks, I pulled over, ran back, and asked how he was doing.

"He's going fast," they answered, "better take us to a spot closer by."

I led up the freeway north for seven minutes, then turned west toward the mountains not far from my own house. I pulled off on a dirt road, then on a trail leading along a pipeline, and off again on a track out into the empty desert. Jack's pickup was right behind me.

I turned off the truck lights and got out. A wedge of gray dawn was easing into the eastern horizon. You could see lights way off in the valley but there were no houses or lights nearby. A single saguaro and a few scrawny mesquite trees were visible through the morning gloom. I knew a tiny wash ran through and watered the saguaro and mesquite; I sometimes came out here myself to spend the night when I needed a little space. It wasn't all that bad a place to die.

I built a little mesquite fire and put a folding chair next to it. We helped Ed get into it; he wanted to sit up by the fire for a while. After a few minutes, Ed said he was ready to get into the sleeping bag. We all came over and said good-bye, then backed off again. Clarke got in the sleeping bag with him and we waited. And waited.

He got better.

"Sometimes the magic doesn't work," he said, as the sun rose into the desert sky.

By midmorning, it appeared that Abbey wasn't quite ready to die. We packed him up and went back to his writer's shack on the edge of a wash draining the Tucson Mountains. Here, Clarke could be with their children; her father, Tom Cartwright, Steve, Jack, and I could alternate shifts during the night. It was comforting to have Steve's impassioned competence. Ed seemed to be a little stronger that night. Again, only a blood clot stood between Ed's living and his dying. Steve said the fresh blood we were dripping into Ed's veins wasn't getting there fast enough. We'd have to get him in somewhere he could be force-fed the blood he needed. Gravity alone wasn't doing the trick because Abbey's veins had collapsed. But going back to the hospital was not part of the deal. I had already pushed as far as I felt decent by arguing for the brutal and humiliating violation of the shunt operation.

We saw him through the night in shifts. We had a bad morning because Ed gagged or coughed and started bleeding again. The day was better. By sunset I was the most hopeful I had been in four days. I had a shooter of Wild Turkey with Ed's sister, Nancy, and his sister-in-law, Susan. A giggle of optimism escaped me because I really thought Ed was going to make it another 20 years. I went home to sleep for four hours in preparation for my midnight shift.

I was alone with Ed most of that night, the last six hours of his life. Mainly, I just sat, watched, and administered the drugs; Compazine to counteract the nausea and gagging resulting from the blood from his throat running down into his stomach; morphine to decrease pain and, hopefully, as a cough suppressant; and Demerol, another opiate, to lessen pain and general discomfort. An IV of 5% dextrose dripped into Ed's veins. I administered the Compazine IV through the intravenous tube, the Demerol could be injected into the muscle or, cautiously, intravenously. The morphine was suppository form.

After my 2 AM sticking of Ed's now atrophying muscles—poking 21 gauge needles into his bony shoulders—I quit injecting him altogether. I had lost heart and couldn't bear to hurt him anymore. Everything except the morphine could go through the IV drip. I didn't want to bother him with these shams of modern medicine or wake him as I had when I injected him with the Demerol. He had opened his eyes then and turned toward me.

"How about that overdose, Douglas?"

Things were quiet for an hour and a half. I still had hope, though fatigue had distanced me from the world. The boundaries between sleep and death, between living and dying, had blurred. It seemed to me Ed was already partway down that corridor into the otherworld; I was trying to follow as best I could. But it was hard. At 4 AM, he started to gag and cough.

Shit. I stepped back into the world of light.

I gave him more morphine, a drink of water, and tried to make him comfortable, but the blood in his stomach made that impossible. I ran the two hundred feet to the house and woke up Steve. This was bad. I ran back to the shack. Ed was sitting up.

"Isn't it about time for that overdose, Douglas?"

"I'll give you what I've got," I replied.

There was no more bullshitting. I drew out far more Demerol than prescribed and mixed it with a suitable dose of Compazine. If he didn't stop coughing and sleep, he'd die no matter what.

I showed him the big syringe loaded with opiate.

"How about a boilermaker, Ed?"

He managed a frail grin. I shot the potent mix into the rubber dripper in the IV. I hoped it was an honest dose. Steve came rushing in and I briefed him. The prognosis was now very grave.

By daylight, the family had been awakened and Ed's doctor arrived. But Ed didn't seem to be there anymore. I fell asleep against the wall, waking every few minutes to look for a miracle. When I saw Steve listen to Ed's heart and then break down, I knew it was all over.

The very last time—it was just before dawn—Ed Abbey smiled was when I told him where he was going to be buried, and I smile too when I think of this small favor, the final duty, this last simple task friends can do for one another:

The rudimentary shovel work, this sweaty labor consummating trust, finally testing the exact confirmation by lying down in the freshly dug grave to check out the view: bronze patina of boulder behind limb of palo verde and turquoise sky beyond branch of torote; then receiving a sign—seven buzzards soaring above joined by three others, now all ten banking over the volcanic rubble and riding the thermal up the flank of the mountain, gliding out and over the distant valley.

4 BURYING HAYDUKE

Then it was back to the desert country of southwest Arizona, that harsh, dry region we all loved, the most important thing Ed Abbey and I ever shared—the Cabeza Prieta. We drove through washes lined with mesquite and desert willow, over creosote-studded bajadas, past cholla and ironwood, driving west with Ed packed in dry ice in the bed of the truck. The sun was low on the horizon. Toward the west, the colors of sunset clashed with the absolute black-and-white expanse of basaltic boulders peppered by ghostly brittlebush. As far as the eye could see—distant ranges a hundred miles into the setting sun—there was not a human sign, no roads, trails, or power lines; only the faint evening breeze stirred in this landscape.

In the fading light, Steve, Jack, Tom, and I gathered around a hole dug into a rise overlooking a great valley, taking turns at pick-axing the steel-hard caliche desert soil. Nearby under the thin shade of a saguaro cactus, lay a body bag camouflaged by an Army poncho liner. The digging proved impossible because of a limestone cap rock, and we had to give up and seek out another place to lay our friend to rest. I was having an ominous argument with Jack over what I considered the execution of Abbey's last request concerning the gravesite. Jack was my good friend but this had not been an easy week, and Ed's written burial instructions were, I thought, quite explicit.

The next morning I found exactly the right place to plant old Ed. The desert air seemed charged with a rare crisp purity. Though illegal grave digging is urgent business, I nonetheless seized the moments between shovel scoops to savor this last day on earth with my friend. Steve dug away and, finally, I lay down in the freshly dug grave to make certain it was suitable; the ten circling buzzards confirmed my choice. I felt good, comfortable with our collective duty to Ed. I looked over the desert vastness around me and picked out a dozen possible walking routes to unknown destinations, the currency of adventure.

We carried Ed's body over the rugged ground, and I was shocked at how light he seemed, light as a cloud, mist on a hill. He might have flown away. During the days previous, I had developed a confusing attitude concerning the dead, an outlook perhaps bordering on madness but partly understandable considering the circumstances. The lines between life and death blurred for me. I wasn't sure the dead would stay dead. They might just get up and walk away or disappear.

When no one was looking, I gently felt Ed's nose through the body bag (just to make sure he was still there). That aquiline Abbey beak was there all right. He hadn't gone anywhere.

I had to do this several times, secretly, to reassure myself.

We lowered Ed into the hole. It went quickly. I picked up a black vulture feather for an offering, but there was no time for ceremony. The four of us were not of one mind, nor were we all entirely comfortable with the job. After all, this was illegal transport of a body not officially certified as dead. We were trespassing without permits on land where it was illegal to inter anyone. The dirt was caved back in and covered with natural boulders that were carefully placed with the patina side up and the caliche stains down. It was done. The real Hayduke was buried.

5 COMING DOWN

With Ed Abbey planted safely in his new home on the shore of a great wilderness, poised for a brave beginning across that immense gap between death and rebirth, Tom and Jack packed up and headed back to Tucson. Steve and I waited a while, sprucing up the burial site, pouring Mexican beer and a couple shots of Wild Turkey over the quartzite boulder that marked the head of the grave. Finally, Steve returned to camp; I stayed behind to erase all sign of our presence.

For more than an hour with a succession of creosote-branch brooms, I swept the area clean of every sign of human footprints. It was exceedingly unlikely anyone would stumble across our tracks. People came here seldom and the nearest human habitation was many miles distant. Still, I couldn't allow for even the slightest possibility of some authority catching wind of an illegal grave in the desert and ordering it dug up. Its privacy was my trust, and after four days and nights of dying and two more of burying I had become fanatical. Fatigue had infused my grave custody with a bit of crazy determinism, and it was dangerous. If somebody had showed up with a god-damn shovel, I'd probably have shot the son of a bitch. There would have been more graves.

I trudged alone down the slope to a big wash lined by palo verde and desert willow, my work finished. I was coming down fast. The big cacti puzzled me; for a moment, I thought I might be in Vietnam. I felt lightheaded and ready to pass out; the adrenaline-fueled vigil over death and illegal burial was through.

The wash disappeared into a brushy defile crisscrossed by tracks of coyotes, kit fox, ringtail and bobtail cat, deer, javelina, and a single sheep. For some reason I didn't want to go in there; a touch of fear tugged at my throat. I looked down the arroyo and, just for a second, thought I could see figures coming and going, descending, disappearing into the desert sands. It was crazy, but I believed it might be a portal to the underworld.

Also, I suddenly didn't know where I was. Probably not Utah, I thought. Certainly not Montana. This total, temporary disorientation had happened before; three, maybe four times in my life. I was unsure of the world, and of what to do.

I managed to gather dry grass and twigs and start a fire.

I felt bewildered and vulnerable. Ed was gone. The world was wide-open. I thought of the glib wisdom of certain psychological literature concerning the passing of a father or mentor, the terrible freedom of there being no one left to judge. Daddy dies and, in the paternalistic void, anarchy and possibility run amuck. With my own father, these issues had not come up. But with Ed, a patriarchal haze often clouded the friendship. Now I was all alone.

But there was something else, triggered by squeezing Ed's nose, something ancient and terrifying and almost hallucinatory that scared the shit out of me, that had been lurking in the deepest corners of my soul, something which now reached for recognition in the clear desert light. I was trying to sort out the elusive feeling of tracking the dying into death and the dreamlike quality of trying to bring back the dead who were themselves, it seemed, trying to return to us in dreams and in life.

All the time I had spent in war, or in training for war, as a Green Beret medic, all my experience in emergency rooms and trauma wards, crept back to me, along with the drowned I had pulled from swollen rivers or from under logjams, body bags hauled off mountains and glaciers—the dead, I could see them. All this raced back to me in those hours after the burial. I followed the trail and scent of death through blind corridors of my life, places I had blacked out with grief or denial or booze, places that confused, terrified, and beckoned, these lyrical gardens of frightening illumination and olfaction.

At the bottom of every dark journey of my life lay this horrifying uncertainty: Am I alive or did I die, and is this but a dream of life?

Maybe I was actually killed in one of the car wrecks—there were several—or drowned in a frigid river. Perhaps I had fallen to my death on a snowfield or died by bullet, mortar, rocket, or grenade decades ago in Vietnam and this day is but illusion. I wasn't sure.

Insanity.

I knew I should try to do something, weep or run through the desert or scream for help from Steve. But I just sat in the dry wash wondering if I were alive and in the real world.

I moved my hands, touched my nose and mouth, ran my fingers over my shoulders and my chest. I could feel my heart beating. I touched my beard and balding head, confirming my age. I felt my legs and feet, as I had another night in these parts, hiking alone across the Cabeza Prieta when I got bit by a rattlesnake and fell asleep at the fire, thinking I might die. I woke in the dark with the fire burned down, uncertain if I was still alive or not and feeling my body, touching the bite to feel how much it had swollen. Now, in another desert wash, I felt my calves and ankles. Everything seemed to be there.

The way out of this nightmare, I told myself, is to get a grip on your own mortality. Take a lesson from old Abbey, and cut a deal with death, because sure as hell that's where the train is headed.

A raven croaked from beyond the wash, over a desert bajada littered with basalt boulders, and slowly I became aware of other sounds: the sweet gargle of phainopepla, the laughter of Gambel's quail, the buzzing of bees at red trumpets of the hummingbird bush. High above circled four buzzards. I watched them. Ed had wanted to be reincarnated as a turkey vulture. He will have lots of company here, I thought. It was a good place to end up, a good resting spot for old Hayduke.

That Hayduke had in another way been born in the Cabeza Prieta, where I first learned about Abbey's book and where we planned our great walks. I remembered the one we took just before he finished *The Monkey Wrench Gang*. Of the dozen or so trips we took together out into the Cabeza, it remains my favorite, and was part of the long circular journey that had drawn me back here to bury Ed under a vault of desert sky. We had passed right through here, fifteen years ago, Ed and I, with my collie dog Larry, in my old pickup on our way to the Pinacates.

At that time, Ed and I were without families and had spent a sniffling, lonely Christmas Eve at a topless bar in Tucson drinking whiskey. Thinking we ought to be able to improve on that one, we packed up and drove 150 miles west into the Cabeza Prieta. We sipped beer all the way from Three Forks and were a tad plastered by the time we hit Charlie Bell Pass. We got my '66 Ford pickup stuck several times, creeping down the treacherous road, hanging up the rear bumper of the truck, jacking it up in the dark, rocking it free, and then dropping down into the Growler Valley.

At Charlie Bell Well, we got out for a piss break. We stumbled around in the dark using a flashlight until we found the Indian petroglyphs carved on basalt boulders. We knew about them. There were carvings of sheep and of shapes that looked like thunderheads with lightning and rain pouring down. This was the place where the ancient Hohokam waited for the first rain of the monsoon season on their way south to the Sea of Cortez to collect the sea shells they carved into their dream animals. We found one carving that looked like a thunderbird. Ed thought it was probably a vulture and said that when he died he planned to come back as a turkey buzzard. There was true magic here. Ed believed this Indian rock art of the Southwest would someday be recognized as a great Native American art form, as significant as the stunning Magdalenian paintings of horses and bison in Late Paleolithic caves in France and Spain.

Ed said the most magnificent and impressive rock art on this continent was in a place called Barrier Canyon in Southeast Utah. "Go there and see it," he said.

I pledged I would—a promise I kept.

We continued on around the north end of the Granite Mountains where we got stuck again, finally crawling into our sleeping bags shortly after midnight.

The next morning, we walked off our hangovers exploring the north edge of the Granites. To the north, the dark outline of the andesitic Aguilas—the "Eagle Mountains"—loomed on the horizon. Neither Ed nor I had been there. The Aguilas might have been the wildest part of the Cabeza. There were supposed to be a lot of bighorn sheep in there. We decided we'd have to explore the Sierra Aguila some time when there was a lull in military activity, since that country was a live-fire bombing range.

We followed Growler Wash where it bent around the north end of the mountains and then turned south. There was nothing and nobody for 50 miles. The white flag of an antelope bounced toward a gap in the Bryant Mountains.

"You know, you could walk straight east through that pass all the way to Ajo," said Abbey.

"Yeah, it'd be clear sailing all the way to Charlie Bell. You could water up there," I answered.

"That's a hike we need to take sometime," he noted, "this driving pickups is for wimps."

Later that day, Ed, Larry the dog, and I drove west through the Mohawk Valley to Eagle Tank in the Sierra Pinta, where we would first plan our longest treks, the greatest walks of our respective lives, our solo hikes across the Cabeza Prieta.

Ed took his first trek in December of 1981, entering the Cabeza from the northwest, next to the Copper Mountains, and exiting on the Camino del Diablo at Bates Well in Organ Pipe Cactus National Monument. The solo hike took a week and covered 110 miles. I know because I stumbled across his tracks and followed them for 30 miles before veering off on a route of my own that would end up here, near Ed's grave. I was also taking one of my seven big walks across the Cabeza Prieta, my second, and didn't know Ed was out here. Though we both took them alone, they seem now like the major shared currency of our lives.

In this driest of American deserts, you had to carry everything on your back, including food and water sufficient to see you across up to 45 mile stretches of bone dry terrain. If you can't find the water holes, you die.

Nearly every winter, for almost a decade, beginning in the late seventies, I walked alone across this place at solstice time, until my children were old enough to know what Christmas was. I did it to walk off the belly fat and get a handle on my life when it seemed out of control: since by then, my war sickness had made its appearance. Three of those big walks, covering 120, 140, and 135 miles, ended up right here in this wash. Only one of my big walks across the Cabeza was cut short and that was because at Senita Tank, in the middle of nowhere, Ed and Clarke Abbey crawled out of a wash. They had driven in with their pickup, and I rode out with them. Otherwise, during the seven walks that averaged ten days each, I didn't see a single human on the ground (I disregard the military planes). Abbey tried another great walk across the Cabeza in March of 1984 but had to abort after four days because of illness.

These journeys, centerpieces of our desert solitaires, were conceived right there with old Hayduke at Eagle Tank back on New Year's Day, 1974.

It's been a while since I've taken one, years, since before Ed died. Someday I'll take another, maybe my last. Still, we managed to do all the ones we planned but one, the one down along the "Eagle Mountains," through the bombing range.

Maybe I'll do that last walk for both of us.

I poked a mesquite stick farther into the fire and lay down in the cool sand of the wash. Hayduke was full circle. Most of him, in any case. Gone and buried. The real-life George was still here. Sort of. I was still confused. I felt that I was none of the people whose mask I had worn: grizzly man, father, earth warrior, husband, Hayduke, drunk, Green Beret medic, nature boy. I was merely the tired, chunky, balding man eyed by buzzards as he squatted, filthy from grave digging, in the arroyo by the fire, dimly desiring a new life.

The aging warrior was weary of his own predictable behaviors and emotional tightness fueled by senseless rage. I detested this legacy of anger and, aware that its deeper roots lay in war, knew it wouldn't be easy to shake. I wanted to stalk this elusive center, using my primitive tools of self-examination—walking, solitude, wildness—to reach back in and touch the source of my wound. Of course I was a poor candidate for a meditative life. My life was a catalogue of psychotic twitches and addictions: official government-sanctioned post-traumatic stress disorder, a combat disability, borderline attention deficit disorder, marginal Tourette's syndrome, occasional depression, a borderline schizoid paranoiac, a history of alcohol abuse. Guys like that don't become Zen masters.

I beat myself up over the monotony of the issues, their tedious persistence in my life. I knew the best answer to this complaint did not lie in conventional therapies but in walking the wild country, the original habitat of mankind; this homeland was indispensable to life, change, and to hope.

This was why I was squatting here in this pretty wash lined by giant desert willow trees. In a way, it was the only reason. Ed Abbey had brought me to this primitive belief in the value of wildness. The land was everything; one's own concerns were dwarfed by the immensity of our need for it.

From the tiny fire, I looked out and wondered what spiritual topography to seek when you want to change the declination of your walks? And who and what had been my most trusted guides so far in life? I could do much worse than Ed, that horny, crabby old fart, much like the grizzlies I so loved.

Ed knew the best wisdom came directly from the earth; it runs right up our roots into the spirit. Walk on. The feet will inform the soul.

From the bench, I see unending Himalayan peaks, glaciers, more plateaus and summits, the gray space of valleys between. The country is so immense, you feel you can see the whole world. At twenty thousand feet, clouds roll down the northeastern shoulder of Dhaulagiri and unfurl across the broad expanse of scree. There is still snow on the ground. In the vaporous gaps between engulfing pulses, the weather cracks and I catch glimpses of towering glaciers and distant peaks. The pass must be just out of sight, up the faint footpath winding through the rotten talus. A gasp of blue bursts through the wall of gray like a shotgun blast. A dozen male grandalas flit among patches of ground-hugging phlox. The little bug-eating thrushes drift away in the fog. I'm not even sure I saw them. Nepal is like a dream.

In the thin air, I remember the giddy faintness of Ed Abbey's mind during the last months of his life. He was low on blood. The doctor said he had lost half of his normal volume during one hemorrhagic weekend in 1989 when the veins in his throat ruptured. The resulting anemia starved his brain of oxygen and produced an odd, insular, and cranky humor. He was very funny, which tended to make him misanthropic toward adults and gentle with children. He knew the end was near, and that he was forever free of the conceits of culture.

I am the oldest by a decade of our little group here in the Himalayas and old enough to be a grandfather to the youngest of the Sherpas. They are probably wondering if I will make it, if I'll die up here and make a lot of trouble for everybody. They might have reason for concern. I do have symptoms of hypoxia: a mild altitude headache, some sleep dysfunction, and obvious loss of short-term memory.

I drift through the fog, one foot, then the other. I am too low on oxygen to feel the pain in my feet or back. I hum a Gershwin tune and for a moment imagine myself like old Ed with half his blood leaked out, a half-wit breathing half my accustomed air. My dull brain does the computations: at 18,000 feet, the atmospheric pressure is almost exactly half of that at sea level. Normal oxygenation of human tissue is dependent on the concentration of oxygen in the lungs, the hemoglobin in the blood, which combines with it, and sufficient red blood cells to carry it to the cells that need it. Something like that. The body acclimates to high altitude somewhat by making more red blood cells but that takes time and mine haven't hatched yet. Breathing half the air probably equals losing half your blood.

So, this is what it's like: Abbey's bloody wit at the end. My hypoxic cerebral circuitry walks upward joking with itself.

The sea of billowing clouds calms, the space between waves of fog lengthens. The heavy, damp weather begins to thin out. I can see a faint horizon ahead, a dim saddle in the enormous ridgeline. The pass. Only another five hundred feet of climbing to go.

The clouds to the southwest separate for a couple minutes, revealing ice fields buttressing Dhaulagiri. In the gray distance, two ravens, four choughs, and a kite fly through the hole. The birds look ominously dark in this black-and-white landscape.

I concentrate on the climb, watch my boots and try to regulate my breathing. I pause frequently, panting to catch my breath. My pack is nearly empty; the others—worried they'd end up with an unwieldy corpse weighing many stones to pack out—thankfully saw to that. I hope I'm up to this. The only way to know is to keep going.

The upside to this is that walking puts me back in touch with my aging, aching body. This takes a few days, about four, in my experience, which includes a lot of time hiking alone in wild territory. On solo backpacking trips across the Cabeza Prieta or to the Grizzly Hilton, something starts to happen on the fourth or fifth day. I totally lose my desire for caffeine, booze, sugar, fat, salt, and instead begin to feed my needs in incremental dosages. For instance, I sweat heavily and used to take salt tablets to replace the sodium, which provided way more salt than I needed. Now I wait until the itch for salt surfaces, dip the tip of my finger into a baggie of granulated sodium chloride, and then lick it off until the hunger goes away (always less than you think). Just yesterday, I gently suggested to the three young Sherpa porters, who prepare our food, that they back off on the yak butter, cheese, and canned milk; they are only cooking traditional Tibetan food, of course, but my well-fed, non-third-world body wants grains. It's as if the body consciousness wants me to walk the fat off it, to streamline this much abused corporeal seat of the soul for pure function, using the least drastic means to get the job done.

The sun glints through broken clouds south of Nilgiri. The snow has melted. My wind is good and my head is clear, though I still have a high-altitude headache. I lead our six man team up toward the pass, breathing deeply and blowing out every two steps, keeping the rhythm, making it up as I go—just as Lisa and I had made up the breathing exercises we hadn't practiced when our daughter Laurel was born in Montana a month earlier than we expected. I purse my lips, blowing out against my teeth to maintain back pressure. Somehow, it works and my headache goes away.

The pass is a broad expanse of scree; only the tops of snow-covered peaks loom in the near distance. I can see snowfields on Dhaulagiri, though the summit remains shrouded in clouds. A few hardy species of saxifrage and heather pioneer the scant patches of soil; not much else grows here. We must be just below 18,000 feet as we walk northwest, across the high pass. Finally, Hidden Valley comes into view; a high grassland covering the moraine debris of a U-shaped depression some fifteen kilometers long and a couple of kilometers wide at its broadest. Most of this lovely little drainage lies between 15,000 and 16,000 feet above sea level and contains its own weather; the monsoon clouds parting and rolling around Dhaulagiri maintain a local high-pressure system that keeps the surrounding cumulus at bay. A slot of blue sky hovers over us, hemmed in on all sides by rain clouds. A herd of eight wild yaks graze in the dwarf willows along the lower creek. Somewhere down there are blue sheep and snow leopard. I can feel them.

We take a break. The Sherpas use precious cedar twigs carried from far below to heat water for tea. Al studies the topographic map and picks out routes up and out of Hidden Valley, heading west; all entail a bit of glacier travel or technical rock work. Dennis goes off by himself, picking over the scree and primitive soils. He squats and plucks a piece of quartzite from the loam. He opens his Arapaho Indian medicine bag and adds the quartz stone. Later, he tells me this is the first time he has opened the sacred bag in many years.

Ed is again on my mind; one of the reasons I came here was to come to terms with dying, to make a friend of death, as Ed did. Not that I think I'm going to die anytime soon. I have simply reached that stage in my life. Ed died slowly after four days of alternately leaking and gushing blood from his throat. My companions here, students of Eastern philosophy—who are patiently trying to enlighten me in matters Buddhist—tell me the throat is supposed to be the seat of communication and that speech is the link between the peaceful divinities of the heart and the wrathful deities of the brain.

Frankly, neither Ed nor I were all that great at communication and there was plenty of wrath along the way. He was the most difficult close friend I ever had. Though Ed and I both laughed at the frail psychology of those who spent half their lives getting over their relationships with their fathers, there was a touch of Old Testament paternalism in our brotherhood. That this most masculine of friendships would eventually sprout a celebration of openness and vulnerability is an odd result. The message that I loved old Ed and always did had to wait until four days before he died to finally get delivered.

Ed Abbey had little use for organized religion, but nevertheless believed there were observable guidelines for living, an accessible wisdom residing in the land, often tapped into by native peoples observing the natural world for the appropriate cycle of life. Ed had always called the Taoist philosopher, Chuang-Tzu, the first anarchist. Tao or Dao, means the Way or the Path, and this image (the nature of truth as trail) is far older than literature. All ancient and traditional people had a Path and knew the seeking of the Way, and these instructions were often remarkable in their similarities. It is the organic way for humans to know and think about their place on earth. For Ed, the Way was wild nature, and the Path was a person walking in it utterly attentive. That place was our original habitat, the wilderness, the Heart of the Lotus, and it was less a path than an off-trail bushwhack. "When your mind is empty like a valley," said Lao-tse, "then you will know the power of the Way."

Below, the bright light of Hidden Valley shimmers off slabs of schistoid talus. The white brilliance beckons.

6 ABBEY'S COUNTRY

Some weeks after burying Ed Abbey, I crossed over the Arizona border into southeastern Utah, into the land where Ed got his first dose of desert solitaire, the place that started it all. Though it was night by the time I hit Monument Valley, I could make out the looming rock spires piercing the dark sky. I was driving at night because my old Honda Civic had been overheating and because the federal law enforcement community had just swooped down on the conservation movement, arresting the leaders of Earth First!. The same morning of the bust, the FBI came looking for me at my home in Tucson. I was away and intended now to stay out of touch for a while. So I was sliding across the state border under cover of darkness.

Just in case: I was entirely unimportant to the movement, but the Feds were nonetheless at my doorstep.

Independently, I received a rating decision from the Department of Veterans Affairs Regional Office for an "entitlement to a service related disability of 50% for post-traumatic stress disorder (PTSD)" based on "Chronic adjustment disorder." Some of the criterion sounded familiar.

> Occupational and social impairment…due to such symptoms as: depressed mood, anxiety, suspiciousness, panic attacks (weekly or less often), chronic sleep impairment.…

The list went on, including the paranoia that fed directly off the FBI bust.

I hadn't paid much attention to the pattern of these symptoms until just after Ed Abbey died. Although I had experienced them from the day I returned from Vietnam, it never occurred to me to seek benefits for a condition I believed inescapable and, under the circumstances, quite unexceptional. All wars had their post-combat syndromes, and it seemed a bit indulgent to complain about my own. I was directly challenged in this view by two older, wiser men: a mutual friend of Ed and I, Peter Matthiesson, and my old pal Tom Cox, who counseled at the hospital and had talked me into visiting the VA Medical Center in Tucson. There I learned I wasn't nearly as unique or alone as I had imagined myself to be. I functioned well enough to keep the lid on the worst aspects of this syndrome, though my incessant rage at government and authority abraded all relationships and this hostility wore at my marriage. The symptoms would worsen during times of stress or during one of our "limited wars" in Iraq or Afghanistan, eventually becoming so severe my children would be eligible for health and educational benefits.

Let me be clear: I wouldn't trade my time in Vietnam for anything. The war prepared me, hardened me, for the only life I wanted or that I felt was subsequently possible. At the same time, the syndrome known as PTSD was real; it permeated daily life. It was an inescapable trade-off: for me, to fit back into society meant living a half-life, devoid of significant passion.

In the little Japanese hatchback, I had enough camping gear, water, gas money, weapons, simple food—cans and dried goods—to hold out in red rock backcountry for a month without reentering the world of phones and electronic banking that would send a paper trail back to Tucson where the Feds might pick up on it. My wife and children approved of the plan to travel to southern Utah and hide out on the land until they could join me when school got out. That gave me about three weeks to kill, which was just fine with me. I never got tired of walking over this harsh wild land, exploring its sandstone canyons and juniper-studded mesas. My investigative method would be simple: I would live on the land as humans always had, by "camping out."

In this landscape, Abbey hatched *Desert Solitaire*, positioned *The Monkey Wrench Gang* and George Washington Hayduke. Earth First! grew out of this legacy, and somewhere, apart from all this, Peacock fit in—in view of the current FBI bust and my emerging infirmity, I wanted to figure out where.

I started down a long grade that ended in a sharp corner at the bridge over the San Juan River at Mexican Hat. I guessed it was about 2 AM. I drove another half hour, past the Moqui Dugway and Garden of the Gods turn-off. There was no one on the road. I downshifted and chugged the little four-cylinder car up a steep grade. A sheer sandstone wall reached up a thousand feet blacking out the stars in the eastern sky. I climbed through a notch, the summit of Comb's Ridge. I was home: Abbey's Country.

Halfway down the east side of Comb's Ridge, I turned off on a dirt track that crossed the ripped up old highway and dead-ended out on the slickrock. I inched the Honda over the bedrock and parked behind a lone juniper tree. I knew about this place from Ed. This was one of his oldest camps from forty years ago. It was here he started walking the canyons, where he first saw and lived his own legend.

Just before 1950, on a long holiday away from the University of New Mexico at Albuquerque, Abbey and a friend drove Ed's old Chevy to the end of the pavement at Blanding, Utah. From there they took the rough, dusty road south to Bluff where they turned west along the northern bench above the San Juan River. The road disappeared into Butler Wash, and Ed thought they must be getting pretty near the end of the known world. They climbed up the stark bedrock slope of Comb's Ridge—an improbable uplift of sandstone, the result of active geologic tectonics on the relatively stable Colorado Plateau—passing within a quarter of a mile of where I was now camped, to a notch looking off into space. Abbey took one look and was hooked forever. What he saw was a landscape totally new to him.

Abbey hesitated to call what he saw beautiful because there was nothing in it to comfort civilized notions of beauty, nothing pastoral and green, nothing productive or fruitful, no pastures for cows, flowing streams, fields of corn, rustic cabins, no patches of forest, or nice snow-capped mountains. What Ed saw was rock, red and warped and folded and corroded and eroded, all very eccentric, with maroon buttes, purple mesas, blue plateaus, and gray dome-shaped mountains far away in the west. Except for the treacherous, impossible track of the road switchbacking down a thousand feet to Comb's Wash, there was no sign of human life. But for a few cottonwood trees in the bottom, he could make out nothing alive in the silence and heat of this savage desolation.

Ed found it infinitely fascinating. More than fascinating. It was a land of second chances, like a deathbed reprieve. The slickrock was a grown-up's dream of childhood discovery and exploration and, by and large, no one knew about it.

During the 1950s, Abbey remained the desert mystic, pouring over the tightly bunched lines on topographic maps of southern Utah as others studied scripture. He sat on the rim of a mesa for three days trying to have a vision but got hungry and saw God in the form of a beef pie. The names had irresistible magnetism: Grand Gulch, Recapture Canyon, Wolf Hole, Fiddler's Green, Slickhorn Canyon, Bear's Ears, Bug Park, No Man's Mesa, Big Bench, Dandy Crossing, Pucker Pass, or Mollie's Nipple.

Years later, he acquired a pickup and returned to Comb's Ridge on the north end passing Zeke's Hole through Comb's Wash, which looked like a form of paradise to Ed, and on to Cedar Mesa and the south slope of the Abajos.

His fascination, the draw of this land for him, never ended. He found work with the National Park Service at Arches, wrote *Desert Solitaire*, and had a hard time thinking of any other place as home. "By this land, I mean southeastern Utah: the canyon lands;" he wrote, "Abbey's country."

Back in Ed's old camp, I kindled a tiny fire of sagebrush root and juniper twigs. It was about an hour until daybreak. I needed some sleep. When I woke, I'd pack up and think about finding a more remote camp. I wanted to revisit a few of Ed's old haunts, taking time for solitude and reflection. What I had in mind was to camp on Comb's Ridge, go look for a lost Anasazi city, then go north to Lavender Canyon in Canyonlands National Park.

All of those places today are uninhabited and fairly wild, roadless, rarely visited except by range cattle or their cowboys. Nobody lives there now. The irony is that a thousand years ago, and before, there were people all over the place. Humans have roamed these purple mesas for at least 11,000 years. Near here, big-game hunters speared now-extinct mammals with their fluted points. Then, for thousands of years, Archaic hunter and gatherer people roamed these rims looking for game and collecting wild plants. By the time of the birth of Christ, Basket Makers farmed in the bottoms and on the mesas, leaving pit houses, corrugated pottery, and magnificent rock art wherever they traveled. The cliff dwellers, the Anasazi, occupied pueblos or rock rooms and kivas tucked in alcoves under the slickrock rims until near the end of the thirteenth century when a prolonged drought caused them to relocate. These people sustained a relationship with slickrock country for thousands of years. The land was the bridge between human cultures, living and prehistoric, and our link to the nonhuman communities; it is what we hold in common. The beauty and strength Abbey found in this harsh landscape and the way the ancients lived in it were linked.

The next afternoon, I packed to move ten miles up the ridge, far enough so I couldn't hear noises from the nearest road. First, I wanted to visit a particular hill where I'd watch the moonrise.

Perched upon a bench above the San Juan River was a sandstone butte, steep on three sides but accessible from the west. Scrambling up a series of short cliffs and ledges, I reached for a handhold and pulled myself up a chest-high shelf. I brushed myself off and took the remaining ten steps to the summit of the butte.

Cobblestone debris and a gritty soil covered the rounded summit. I could hear Canada geese honking in the dusk down on the San Juan. The broad cap of the butte was dimpled with big saucer-shaped depressions fifteen to twenty feet across.

These craters were the sunken remains of kivas, the round roofs collapsed. The surface of the butte was strewn with potsherds and flakes of agatized wood and Brushy Basin chert. In the dim light, I could make out black-on-white pottery. There were perhaps a dozen circular depressions spread over the top of the butte; there were no other rooms or features, just kivas.

The blood-hued globe of the full moon, an orange bulge, appeared on the horizon behind Montezuma Creek. Geese honked again from the river. I could hear the distant thump of a grasshopper pump from the San Juan oil field. Otherwise, the hush of night embraced the land. I thought about all the material—stones, water, pottery, timber, chert—hauled up here by the Anasazi. There were no ruins or village sites nearby. All the stuff brought here was for ceremonial functions.

I considered this butte a sacred site, a notion of land use not generally given much modern credence but appropriate here in slickrock country. At least, it was practical here to look for a spiritual component in physical places that were repeatedly sought out by humans, throughout the centuries, as places in which to perform ritual acts. These contexts include natural features—mountains and monoliths like the Black Hills, Spider Rock, Devil's Tower or Mount Shasta, sandstone cathedrals, red rivers cutting slots in chocolate rock—as well as man-made relics, such as the ruins of Mexico and the Southwest, the

Medicine Wheel of Wyoming, or the sites of the American Indians' rock art.

This country had been sacred to the Ancients centuries before Ed discovered it. The land had been a partner in my serious human relationships, marriage, parents, sister, children, and close friendships. I believed wisdom and a key physical balance resided in these canyons, buttes, and green mesas and that you could sometimes tap into it by walking over the country with an open mind. Abbey drew heavily from the slickrock source and here formulated his wilderness ethic.

I also wanted to journey back to the origins of my friendship with Ed to remember who I became after Southeast Asia. Since the war, problems with intimacy touched all my relationships. I maintained a marriage by working in the woods and by staying out of the house half of the year. I had some regrets: with friends like Ed I had been inexcusably hard-assed. But that no longer mattered. Cranky or not, it had been a friendship. In the roots of that friendship lay the beginning of my life after Vietnam, the crazy time foreshadowing the creation of George Hayduke. Later, with our children, it got easier. But I could never leave the wild woods; I would, like Abbey, forever be balancing love of friends and family with solitary walks in the wilderness. Solitude is the deepest canyon we ever traveled.

The next day I made my camp on Comb's Ridge, in a little depression behind the dunes under a big cedar out of sight of the valley and the dirt road that ran through it. I pitched the tent, started a tiny fire, and sat on the bedrock in front of the fire looking out under the juniper boughs to the distant rolling valley broken into provinces by the sheer red rock walls that rose randomly into great mesas, buttes, and standing rocks. The difference between this remote desert region and other areas of significant prehistory, such as the places of my boyhood in Michigan, is that this land looks unchanged:

the macro-view remains the same. You look out over this country and you see what the ancients saw. The communities are the same. Only the individuals—trees, plants, animals, humans—change.

A huge bird landed in a cottonwood a quarter mile to the southeast. I sat back and brought my binoculars up: a bald eagle settled in for the night. I pushed a big juniper log onto the fire. The flames leapt, the log threw sparks out into the night, the popping wood interrupting the deep silence of the land.

The sun caught the tent shortly after daybreak. The air was crisp and cool. I packed up a stuff sack with day hike items and headed straight up the ridge. Within a few minutes, I had left the dunes behind and entered an angular world of slickrock. This is the best rock on earth to walk on, I thought. The clean abrasive surface of cross-bedded sandstone invites the feet. Rain-scoured sandstone reaches up to bite the boot. I climbed up the angle. The improbable block of Comb's Ridge is an uplifted slab of slickrock less than two miles wide and thirty-five miles long tilted on its side. Friction climbing these slabs for any length of time distorted my perceptions: the world seemed skewed, far-off canyons listed over on their sides, the soaring redtail flew into space, water sometimes ran uphill. The rock propelled you upward efficiently; there was no slipping. You felt you could walk forever.

Comb's Ridge itself defied mapmaking, at least in terms of self-location. The uplift is a snake of rock thirty miles long, longer if you measure the section south of the San Juan River, running due north, and about a mile and a half wide. It is gently tilted up on the east and falls off steeply into Comb's Wash on the west. The total relief is about a thousand feet, and vertical four- and five-hundred-feet cliffs guard much of the western escarpment. The crest of the ridge in profile is an endless undulation of peaks and troughs, which looks much like a giant comb with coarse teeth. You learned the ridge by walking over it. The topographic maps were worthless; every canyon looked more or less the same on the map. The squat canyons were often boxed at the upper, westerly end, with few rims or cap-rocks as landmarks. Yet in every canyon there is magic: groves of oak and cottonwood, pools of cool water, hidden granaries, kivas, cliff dwellings, and panels of petroglyphs.

By mid-morning I had rimmed-out, staring at a lip of sandstone dropping off into space on three sides. At the crest of the rim lay a pool of rainwater, a big bathtub of water filling a four-foot hole drilled into the rock by torrential summer rains. I filled my canteen from the water hole, then stripped off my clothes and used the canteen cup to pour rainwater over my head and body washing off the road dust. I lolled away the middle of the day naked on the rim. When the chill afternoon wind picked up, I dressed and returned down ridge toward camp.

The next morning I tried another route, aiming farther north toward a distant overhang I could see with my binoculars from the bottom. I climbed up wind-blown sandstone that leveled off onto a plane of bedrock gently angled toward the blue desert sky. I contoured north into a red rock draw. In the bottom ran a trickle of precious water staining a black streak on the rock. The little gulch deepened into a narrow canyon too steep to climb out of. I bushwhacked up the canyon stepping around water pooled behind juniper roots and in deep tinajas. Sagebrush and acacia tugged at my clothing. The tight short run of canyon widened into a saddle between two ridges bathed in sunlight. The temperature had climbed into the seventies. Beads of sweat clung to the back of my wrist and ran down my forehead.

I climbed up out of the wash and over the rise into another basin to the north and dropped into a large draw, a little valley perched just under the summit of Comb's Ridge. I stepped around a little enclosure, about four feet across, made by eight sandstone slabs on their sides. It might have been a cist or even the top of a kiva. An overhanging wall of sandstone stood as the northern barrier of the canyon. A rubble slope climbed up toward the sky. Large sections of the wall were stained with a bronze patina, dark and lovely against a lighter chocolate brown.

I inched down the saddle to the abrupt backside of the asymmetrical ridge. A line of fist-sized depressions led down the precipitous west side of the ridge. These were Moqui steps carved by the ancients, hand-and foot-holds for climbing the wall. It looked like they descended all the way to the bottom. There must have been something special about this place.

I climbed down to the base of the cliff stained with dark streaks. Petroglyphs of sheep and deer, horned figures and a Kokopelli were etched here and there along the wall. Some of these appeared very old, maybe Basket Maker, especially the horned figures and the one with a crested headdress. A lone figure carved in the rock looked like a scorpion.

I moved along the rubble slope at the foot of the cliff and had almost reached the crest of the ridge again. Just as I was about to turn back, I saw more petroglyphs: dozens of figures, most about six or seven inches tall, walked from two directions across the panel toward a circle with dashed-lines dropping down below it like steps. There were a half dozen images that stood slightly apart, clan leaders maybe, with headdresses and long, hooked shepherd's canes. Some of the figures were carrying torches. The hands and feet of many were accentuated like long fingernails. Some were carrying tear-like objects, ladders and a dead man on a scaffold of some kind. I had never seen anything quite like this: the size and number of figures was unique. The panel appeared to be relatively recent, much younger than the Basket Maker art; yet it seemed to have depicted Anasazi people, not Ute or Navajo whose rock art also adorned cliffs in this region.

I moved back down the rubble slope quietly. I picked up a three-pronged antler dropped by a mule deer. When I got back to the slab-sided cist, I placed the deer antler inside. I then packed up, bushwhacked down another canyon, contouring another mile south back to my camp on the lower flank of Comb's Ridge. I started a tiny fire with my disability entitlement letter from the VA. The page crinkled bronze in the heat, then flamed. I recalled more petroglyphs and another burning letter.

^^^

During fall and winter of 1975, Ed was living in Moab. *The Monkey Wrench Gang* had been published earlier that year. I finished my last season as a Backcountry Ranger for the National Park Service. Earlier that spring, I had begun a project filming the remaining grizzlies in the lower forty-eight. After an autumn of shooting movie film in Glacier Park and making my usual forays in Yellowstone, I returned to Southeastern Utah.

Ed asked me if I wanted to take a hike up Mill Creek, which dumped right into Moab. The drainage grew into a large gulch, deepening into a canyon. We climbed up the slickrock using ancient steps pecked into the rocks to examine a panel of petroglyphs. Images of sheep, deer, and hunters were chiseled into the patina separated by symbols, perhaps of mountains, lightning, or sunrises. We had no idea what it was about though it was clear the story it told was epic and the place special. Below, the little canyon forked into two prongs. At the junction was a boulder covered with carvings of humans with rake headdresses, perhaps feathers, and feather-like appendages hanging from their out-stretched arms as if they were about to take flight. On top of the big boulder were carved meandering lines, which turned out to be an accurate map of the area.

This had become a rough time in our friendship. My weekly behavior was sprinkled with random anxiety reactions every time I heard a backfire or loud discharge. That I was always well armed with knives and handguns was also disconcerting to others. And of course the publication of *The Monkey Wrench Gang* hung like a thin, wet horse blanket over the friendship. In one of our lowest moments, the legal staff of Lippincott & Co. had insisted Ed write a very embarrassing letter to me about how I should consider only the good characteristics of George Washington Hayduke a reflection of Peacock and not the bad parts—the usual unhygienic litigious disclaimer.

I had the letter with me. On top of the boulder carved with the ancient map of the area, at the junction of two great canyons, in the heart of D*esert Solitaire* country, we struck a match and ritually vaporized it. We watched the wind carry off charred fragments, gathered by the laughing waters of Mill Creek. Neither of us ever mentioned this matter, nor the roots of George Washington Hayduke, to the other again.

The origins (built on the foundation of Thoreau, Muir, and Leopold) of our Western modern (post-1970) conservation movement and Ed Abbey's *Desert Solitaire*, were, I believe, at least synchronous and possibly synonymous. Similarly, the more militant branch of wilderness preservation came into being partly because of Abbey's *The Monkey Wrench Gang*. This was especially true of the Earth First! group, whose particular style seemed to fly straight off the pages.

Ed's influence on the American conservation movement ranged across the board, but it was Earth First! in particular that was strikingly effective in broadening the wilderness dialogue. It was this expression of free speech, which threatened powerful corporate and governmental interests in the West (and still does), that the federal law enforcement agencies wanted to silence. Subpoenas to activists were issued like parking tickets. The timing of the FBI's Earth First! bust, following conveniently on the heels of Abbey's death, was hardly coincidental.

The fact that the people who were victims of the FBI were my friends gave me a stake in this debacle. Though these causes and people have always had my heartfelt support, I've never been a movement person; I don't like crowds, and loners don't join groups. At the same time, I consider myself at least as dedicated to saving what's left of the wild earth as any bomb-throwing activist. Other than showing up at the nominal Round River Rendezvous, mailing parties, and fund-raisers with Abbey, however, I kept my usual distance.

^^^

Back on the slickrock, I knew I would help my friends as best I could. Meanwhile, I stoked fires of piñon and juniper each night and poured over topographic maps for places to explore. One of these was a "lost city," an Anasazi ruin nearly untouched by pothunters, a whole class of local and international scum who feed the greed-driven markets of grave robbers called "collectors." This illegal looting of archeological ruins was less a destruction of scientific data than a clear sacrilege of sacred sites. It was one reason I always carried a weapon out here, snuck around like an outlaw in camouflage clothing, and slept in hidden camps with one eye open. If I encountered grave robbers without them knowing I was about, I could always let the law handle it. To surprise a serious pothunter could lead to a bloody shootout. This I wanted to avoid, though I was prepared to go either way.

The big Pueblo village was somewhere up on Big Bench. I'd heard about it from a friend who worked as a salvage archeologist for a highway survey. The ancient city was on a little hill visible from the overlook on the rim above.

I got out my maps and found the knoll. There was an old jeep trail that hadn't been used for years heading out to the promontory. I turned off the paved road, disappeared quickly into the juniper and parked short of a point of land; the old rutted track was too much for the little low-slung Honda. With my binoculars, I walked to the edge of the mesa. Far below was a broad valley with sandstone and clay badlands furrowing the bottoms. A pile of rocks perched upon one of these isolated rises. I brought up the field glasses. Heaps of rocks on a small hilltop formed rectangles and circles. Stacks of stone masonry sat on the edges of the steeper hills. It was an Anasazi city.

Packing up for the day, I dropped down the five or so hundred feet over the rugged scree and big slabs of the valley sides. I crossed much deer sign and the track of a small mountain lion. When I got to the bottom, I realized I was upon a very large, undisturbed Anasazi pueblo. There were perhaps thirty rooms and twenty kivas, mostly on the south side of the little city. It had rained recently and the clay layers were gumbo—sticky bentonite soil—so I avoided walking on the ruin; walking would hasten erosion. The valley was abandoned now except for a few range cattle. I couldn't complain much; empty land was an antidote to despair.

An isolated hill jutted out into the western side of the valley. Even from a quarter of a mile away, I could see it was covered with rock walls. It was another pueblo, much bigger than the first. This site, largely occupying a secure hilltop, extended into the flat where stone walls outlined the remains of a fortified plaza guarded by two towers. Evidence of an ancient road ran up and down canyon from the abandoned village. There were perhaps fifty or more rooms and at least thirty kivas within the complex. I walked over several collapsed kivas; I could see down inside, see the roof beams and space beneath. I circumnavigated the pueblo; there were a couple of pits in the midden, but this site was otherwise undisturbed.

This was a place I wanted to bring my children. Laurel and Colin would love this lost city. I remembered the leap of mind undisturbed archeological sites held for me as a child. For the eleven-year-old boy, looking for arrowheads in the muddy fields was like entering unexplored wilderness, and it set the stage for future discovery.

I poked and stumbled about the ruin for another hour. Both Kayenta and Mesa Verde-type pottery littered the ground along with older Basket Maker material. Pieces of grooved axes and a rare ceremonial hoe lay on the deflated bench. I dropped into a gully that was deeply eroded from decades of cattle overgrazing. Lines of rocks marking pit houses fell out of the vertical wall. I turned a tiny bend and saw bones, human bones, eroding out of the bank. A foot away was half a funeral vessel of corrugated pottery. I climbed back up and found a big cottonwood stick, which I used as a pry bar to collapse dirt over the human remains, temporarily reburying the skeleton. Otherwise, I touched nothing.

The weather heated up. The four-cylinder sedan complained loudly. Rattlesnakes were out in the low country and insidious gnats gnawed away at vulnerable places on me during unguarded moments. It was time to move up a few thousand feet to another life zone.

I headed to Cedar Mesa, a largely deserted land now, but the slickrock version of Manhattan during Anasazi times. I climbed a low blunted summit for a view of the country. To the south and east lay the spires of Monument Valley, Shiprock, and, beyond, the great Anasazi Chacoan road system—first pointed out to me by Ed—radiating out of Pueblo Bonito in the upper San Juan Basin of northern New Mexico. Chaco was a religious center. Naturally, as our modern religion is commercial greed, for many years anthropologists assumed these straight roads were trade routes. But they weren't. The ancient roads were spiritual ways, constructed at huge expense during periods of great drought. They were ways of beauty and of human harmony with the land, clear paths to truth and living well on earth, roads emanating from a central source, telling the people the story of who they were.

Ahead lay Natural Bridges National Monument, a National Park Service unit, which once refused Ed Abbey a job because of his FBI record. I stopped and bought a map at the Bureau of Land Management trailer at the head of Grand Gulch, a large canyon system, which dumps into the San Juan River below Mexican Hat. This roadless canyon is a designated "Primitive Area" and is known for its well-preserved prehistoric rock art and ruins dating from Basket Maker and Anasazi times. Any time you designate some place an official park or wilderness or primitive area, you unavoidably hype it. Thus many people come here to hike and backpack. It might be the most popular recreational backcountry in the San Juan Basin.

For me, recreation is an inadequate reason to pollute the wilderness with my own human presence. The wild is too important. I would like to see great chunks of uninhabited country, which we, by voluntary compliance, never enter. And other areas, encompassing most truly wild regions in the lower 48, that we visit only during critical and self-defined times of personal passage, maintaining empty land for our collective spiritual journeys or vision seeking.

That said, I am forever creating quests to justify my numerous wilderness invasions: a search for a lost city or to see the black grizzly or to visit the feral grave or ceremonial cairn of a dead friend, track a jaguar or tiger, sometimes to take an eagle feather to a secret circle of bison and grizzly skulls or to seek out medicinal plants or food. Although this reeks of self-service, I want to imagine this keeps me from bagging random peaks in prime grizzly habitat or taking mindless jogs down a wilderness trial. Witness the rapidly escalating number of incidents of mountain lion attacks on Lycra-clad runners.

Though solitude was what I preferred, I didn't mind sharing the area. I shouldered my pack and started down Bullet Canyon. There was a maintained trail running down this side canyon. On my way down Bullet to the main run of Grand Gulch, I looked up and with field glasses saw a tiny ruin on the rim with huge moons or white circles painted on it. I passed springs, thickets of cottonwoods, panels of rock art, and ruins with pens for domesticated wild turkeys. I passed a place called "Perfect Kiva" and though I knew of two others, more remote and unknown "Perfect Kivas," I stopped and dropped down though the roof, climbing down the piñon pine (tastefully lag-bolted) ladder—a replacement for the original provided by the BLM Primitive Area. I moved around the periphery of the kiva to find the place most comfortable to me. Finding one, I sat in the darkness for a while trying to imagine the people who had sat here before me. Slowly, the spiritual moment yielded to a touch of modern claustrophobia. I climbed back out into the sunlight. Immediately, the tightness went away and I felt better.

I passed two small groups of backpackers in the main canyon, and I sat out the day as far as possible from the trail but still within the canyon. Behind me was a hidden panel of petroglyphs of Kokopellis, the hunchback flute player of the Ancients, their phalluses greatly exaggerated, one growing and becoming a giant serpent.

That night I camped near a site called the "Green Mask" after a haunting shamanistic face, an amazing panel with white painted walls and moons made of real mud and red-dot paintings of women giving birth. Yet the magic escaped me; my heart had left the spontaneity of the moment. I didn't know why but I decided to climb out.

The next morning, I bushwhacked out an unnamed canyon to the east. On the way out, I saw a big bird; a peregrine falcon flying below the rim of windblown sandstone. The falcon flew along an overhang. I followed with my binoculars; suddenly, twelve Anasazi granaries came into view, seven of which still had roofs and great rocks blocking the entrances, untouched since, as modern Pueblos say, "the Wind Blew the Anasazi Away."

I saddled up the Honda and drove south where I camped at the head of Slickhorn Canyon. In the morning, I walked the north rim for a mile then dropped down through the cliffs to a broad shelf running above the side canyon. On a small dirt ledge back up the canyon but below me, two sticks protruded out of a square hole in the ground. A big crack led down to the level of the ladder. It was "the Perfect Kiva." I knew of it from a friend. This kiva was completely intact. Very few people on earth knew it was here and even fewer had visited. Somehow I knew I couldn't enter that holy place.

That night I drank a bottle of red wine in front of a raging fire. After the coals burned down, I crawled into my sleeping bag and edged my mind toward sleep by counting gray whales as they drifted by in the morning fog, forty feet from my daughter's tent on a sand island off the southern coast of Baja.

I woke the next morning with a hangover. I had a headache and felt nauseous from physical and cerebral disorientation. Time to move on. There was supposed to be a method to my walking and it had to do with geography of mind. I wanted to end up in a better spot.

^^^

I packed up and headed out, turning east on the Natural Bridges road, north around the Abajo Mountains and then west, stopping at Newspaper Rock to admire the many grizzly-bear petroglyphs; these sets of Ute, Anasazi, and older bear tracks were, though stylized, clearly griz not black bear. I suspected grizzlies had been the more common bear here along the running creeks and higher in the piñon zones before the arrival of the White Man. At Dugway Ranch, I passed south through the buildings and turned off west on a jeep trail that threaded back into Lavender Canyon. Jeeps could drive all the way up into the canyons—unnecessary and unfortunate travel, I thought. At another time, I might have bitched about having to make the long flat walk in when others arrived in their blazers and broncos. Tonight I didn't give a shit; I squeezed the roll of belly fat under the steering wheel of the Honda; I needed to walk it off. I parked the Honda miles out from the mouth of the canyon and shouldered a big pack, planning to stay out for a few days.

Pink and cream-colored cliffs rose from the valley fill to flank the sand wash, which deepened into a canyon as I walked upstream. The walls grew rapidly. The narrow canyon cut deeply into the core of the Abajo range. Lenses of lavender sandstone adorned the rims of towering benches. Here and there it looked like it might be possible to climb up through the series of ledges to the mesas above.

I passed a little ruin in a side canyon off to the west. An occasional Anasazi granary perched on high inaccessible ledges below overhangs. By and large, ancient settlement in this lovely canyon was not as extensive as in Comb's Wash, Cedar Mesa, or Grand Gulch. Perhaps that was the result of the simple shortage of flat cultivatable land and suitable living sites. But what I was wondering about was beauty. Who would not want to live in a place so lovely?

The place knocked your eyeballs out. The ancients must have seen what we see now: that beauty lies outside culture. The canyon assaulted the senses: the easy and immediate apprehension of the simple classical lines of these earth forms and colors, arrived with the swiftness of an emotion, at light speed. There were no superfluous details. Seeing this brought the organic connection between Ed's slickrock cosmology and the life native people had lived here.

It was easy to see why Ed had admired it, a true gem within a visually high-grade landscape. He believed that beauty in nature is a reflection of the ultimate beauty of the universe, the final explanation of which is composed of a few principles of compelling simplicity. My paternal grandmother, now departed, used to call this straightforward and pervasive beauty the reflection of the light of God.

I had to believe I was tracking some divine signal here because I was having trouble with everything except the beauty of the land. I seemed to be the guy who walked around a lot in wild country looking at stuff without learning much of anything useful about himself. I was filled with a variety of self-loathing I recognized but seldom allowed others to see, a darkness associated with mood swings that took months to turn around. I wondered whether I was on the way up or down. The troughs of these depressions could be real whoppers. My only weapon against them had been to turn antisocial: to be alone either with my children or in the wild.

That night I pitched a tent. The sky had turned stormy. I listened to coyotes in the night. A soft rain woke me about midnight and continued falling until daylight. Coyotes again howled, regrouping after the evening hunt. I thought of the Cabeza Prieta, the desert wilderness in which I had spent the most solitary nights, Ed's new home. For a moment, all deserts became one.

At sunrise, I got up and walked farther up Lavender Canyon, looking up at the sheer cream and rose-tinted cliffs. At a major fork in the canyon, a series of cracks and chimneys led up through the vertical cliffs. I climbed up, marking my difficult route with little cairns.

On top, I walked the pink rim. Below in an inaccessible alcove, sat an Anasazi granary. A pair of ravens dipped and rose along the undulating wave of rock. Redtails soared above. The shadows fell. I walked south on the east rim then cut across the mesa west and followed the lip of the main fork back. I found one little kiva attached to a two-room Anasazi unit—not much evidence people lived here. Maybe it was the lack of game; there was little sign of deer and other game animals on the mesa.

It was getting dark. I needed to climb down four or five hundred feet to my camp below. I followed and dismantled the cairns until they led down a crack widened by runoff. The exposure was incredible; you hung out over a hundred vertical feet. I couldn't believe I had come up that way. A fall could have been fatal. The sun had been down for an hour. A thin film of light lay on the mesa, and I could make out juniper trees on the ledge fifty feet below. In twenty minutes it would be full dark. I carried matches but I didn't want to be stuck on a slickrock ledge for an entire chilly night. The cliff ran north and slightly downhill, then rounded to an overhang, the lip of which wasn't too far above the tops of the trees on the ledge below.

I raced north along the rim, looking for a way down. At one point, I found I could edge over the rounded cliff and climb down another twenty feet. But the drop was a leg-breaking thirty feet, so I kept going. I could barely see. I edged down again. The tops of juniper trees were far out of reach but only ten feet away. I could leap into the branches, hoping the boughs would break my fall. But that might cost an eyeball or worse.

Time was running out. I picked a spot to make my move. Tying on a nylon cord, I lowered my pack, with the binoculars inside wrapped up in my jacket, down by hand. The cord wasn't long enough; the pack hung five feet above the sloping ledge below. I dropped it anyway. Off to my left were a couple of marginal handholds in the sloping sandstone leading to the rounded overhang. A small, steeply sloping ledge lay no more than fifteen feet below. The ledge dropped over a short cliff another six feet into slab rubble, with no big boulders that might bash in my head.

I figured: what the hell. My pack was down there. It was showtime. I inched down the rounded overhang. When I got to the first handhold, I rolled over and faced the cliff. I felt the last hold with my toe. I held myself with both hands and dropped my knee to the toehold. I moved my hands one at a time until I was supporting all my weight with both hands in front of my groin. I slowly lowered my body over the cliff. My legs dangled.

A wave of nausea rose up from my belly; I knew this was stupid, that I had made a mistake. But it was too late. It was a full twenty feet to the rocks below where my broken body would lie if I let go now. Only the narrow sloping ledge lay between me and the rugged ground below. To hit it on the way down, I'd have to swing myself back in under the overhang.

I hung in space for as long as I could—seconds maybe—then made my move. Dropping my left arm, I dangled from my right. I pushed against the cliff and swung my legs out. Not far enough. The second time, I got a better swing. I let go as my legs swung back in and dropped back under the overhang. I hit the tiny ledge with my feet together, knees bent, elbows and forearms in front of my face. I landed hard and immediately rolled on my left side, spreading the impact up along my body—my old paratrooper landing. I kept falling. The momentum rolled me up on the side of my head and I felt the skin going. I dropped over the six-foot cliff on my back moving fast. I swung my feet around in midair and hit the bottom flush and hard on both feet. The blow jarred my teeth and I pitched headlong straight down the slope. I missed the prickly pear cactus and finally stopped when my shoulder slammed into a basketball-sized boulder.

I lay there without moving for several minutes. I knew without rising that my back was a mess but I couldn't feel any fractures or big lacerations. The side of my face was bleeding as were both knees and one elbow. But I was down.

In the dark, I felt my way down, negotiating one small cliff, to the sand run of the bottom of Lavender Canyon. I hobbled north and found my camp.

I built a big fire. My wounds were minor. I had got off lucky in the sixteen-foot jump, breaking the fall by hitting the narrow ledge on the way down. The prudent move would have been to build a fire and wait for daylight when finding a safe route would have been easy. There was plenty of water up there. I could have been killed in the fall or, worse, maimed for life.

But this night I lay next to the fire feeling exceptionally calm. My head had cleared. The letting go and the fall had sobered me. Death was not the enemy of life, I thought, the foe was fear of capturing the truth, fear of true introspection. I had learned that from Ed and tonight the instruction returned with humbling veracity. At the end, you had to release, let go of anger, all grasping and attachment, even desire.

"Let it go, idiot," I heard myself say, sitting alone by the fire in the canyon.

To release, to let go and die the little death, to walk it off, to move forward toward enlightenment even if you can't stretch the emotional parameters of your nature, this was the lesson of the friendship that had started with this place, the slickrock, and had ended in another desert, the Cabeza Prieta.

This would be my last night out in the slickrock. I was beginning to understand the necessity of having come here. It had to do with payback propelled by survivorship: acknowledgment of a debt to Ed, my parents and sister, every uncle and aunt, every friend and comrade who had helped raise me in this tradition, a tribal heritage of wildness. And this legacy was a good one. It was an affirmation of Ed's simple observation that what you do, say, and think each day counts. At the bottom of the daily grind, the risk and duty, lay the gift of generosity.

I awoke at daylight and walked the last two miles back to the Honda. I stuffed my gear in the back seat and fired up the tiny hatchback. I bounced back past Dugout Ranch. I turned up Indian Creek, passed Newspaper Rock, and hit the highway north of Monticello. Turning north, I drove through the big standing rock country, past Wilson Arch, and finally into Spanish Valley. Near the bottom of the grade, I parked below a trail climbing back up to the west.

The trail rose directly up the valley wall to the area known as Behind the Rocks, a wilderness of rock south of Moab and east of the Colorado River. I topped out into a long grassy valley running northwest. I reeked of unwashed clothes and wood smoke. The sun was high above the La Sals; it was about 11 AM.

The long, narrow valley curled up to a little pass, then continued north, a graben draining to the north. I peeled off the trail and began to contour east along the low cliffs. A dark patina covered the lower sandstone face, those zones more protected from rain and wind. I brushed past a juniper and abruptly stopped. I could smell the strong pungency of cat spray, a scent too powerful and pervasive for wildcat. I knew this from experience, having long been familiar with the smell of the common bobcat, and having once had the great fortune of snorting fresh jaguar fragrance in the Sierra Madres and, even rarer luck, the scent of a Siberian tiger on the Bekin River of the Russian Far East. Jaguars didn't live here, so the fetor belonged to a mountain lion. This marker smelled fresh.

I moved along the ledge at the foot of a butte. A line of petroglyphs adorned the cliff face. Kokopelli played his flute beneath four bighorn sheep. A hundred feet down the ledge, a line of mule deer had been pecked into the patina. In the sand below the panel were the clawless prints of a round paw four inches in diameter. The lion. The landscape suddenly grew wilder. It was no longer the recreational place behind the rocks just south of Moab, Utah; the land became what it always had been. It bristled with vitality, with the potency to heal. This was the sign I'd been stalking.

7 BARRIER CANYON

Shortly after finding the mountain lion tracks, I sat in a four-wheel-drive pickup truck driving my wife and two children down a rutted dirt road the color of clotted blood. Clumps of sage and rabbitbrush garnished a treeless landscape. The road led to the rim of Barrier Canyon, which snaked on down to the Green River in southeastern Utah. Up ahead I could see the hazy chasm of the slickrock gorge opening up in the gray distance. I bounced to the end of the road and looked down into the canyon. We all needed some closure after Ed's death and bringing my family here, to this place Ed had told me about, was probably as close as I would come to going to church.

The summer was hot and the air still, though the absorbed heat pouring off the sandstone would soon generate thermals and catabolic winds. Lisa filled two canteens and stuffed snacks for the kids into her day pack. I tossed a few first aid items into my own pack along with a snakebite kit. Almost as an afterthought, I crammed in the Ruger .357 Magnum Ed and I had had our last fight over. Colin Peacock and his sister, Laurel, shouldered small day packs. We started down the steep foot trail into the canyon that held the most significant panel of rock art on the continent. This was my first trip to Barrier Canyon. Ed had come here many times.

The trail descended six hundred feet to a sandy bottom, a meandering desert wash with small pools where the watercourse touched the windblown cliffs. Thickets of willow and tamarisk marked the water holes and yellow princess plume and larkspur delineated the dry bank. This canyon looked the same as hundreds of others I'd seen, but I knew that it was not.

My daughter glistened with perspiration, and I dug in my pack for a water bottle, then handed Lisa my pack and lifted Laurel up to ride on my shoulders. I discovered that my first born was no longer so little, and I recalled my earliest memory of the outdoors: riding on my dad's shoulders during the World War II years, when he led his Boy Scout troops into the Michigan countryside to collect milkweed pods for Navy life preservers.

My son led the way up the canyon, stepping around patches of locoweed and buckwheat. A breeze picked up and cooled our faces. The walking was easy. A pair of ravens croaked, circling near the rim. I could hear white wing doves, pinon jays, and canyon wrens calling from the slopes. Beyond them all, four turkey vultures soared far up in the blue.

Off to the left, we came upon a line of painted figures at the base of the cliff; most were mummy-like with no extremities and bucket-shaped heads, square shoulders, and long tapered trunks painted red or white and red. This was the first of the four panels Abbey had told me about. There were three more in the next two miles. The last one was the Great Gallery.

The second panel was like the first except the figures were bigger, though not quite life-size. To the left of the humanoid figures was a big animal painted black. We thought it might be a mountain lion, but its face looked like that of a large dog.

We passed the third panel. My daughter climbed off my shoulders to have a look and give me a rest. We lingered in the shade of an alcove and watched a red-tailed hawk soar through the blue slot of sky above the red rock canyon. My boy and I took the lead and rounding a right-hand bend we could see, at the far end of the canyon, a great overhang of sandstone that faced the rising sun. We struggled through a thin stand of tamarisk and froze: a hundred yards away, above the floodplain of the wash were life-sized figures with square heads and broad shoulders. We had come to the Great Gallery.

Colin and I waited for the girls to round the bend and signaled them forward. Together, the four of us approached the broad canvas of sandstone descending from a rim four hundred feet up.

We climbed out of the wash and stood below the huge, looming, immobile anthropomorphs painted red, black, and white, though most were dark red. Many of the long tapered figures were elaborately decorated: vertical stripes, snakes, lightning, horizontal bands, and horned head-dresses or crowns of dots. Some had feathers or arcs over their heads. One had a bird beak. Near the humanoid figures were those of birds, dogs, snakes, insects, and small animals. It is art predating the Anasazi and Fremont cultures, yet its antiquity appeared anything but primitive; in all my travels, I had never seen anything quite so powerful.

These compositions had been carefully planned; there was very little superimposition or over painting. Artist-shamans had probably executed the images. The small animals inside the chests or hovering around the heads of these ghostly figures seemed to be spirit helpers, birds signifying the flight of the soul, the empty sockets and deathlike, skeletal motifs looked almost like shamans making the initiatory journey into the underworld.

I stepped back to catch my breath and held my family close. Among ancient and tribal people, those members who acquire "death eyes" from a close encounter with death often undergo ritual scarification to denote their altered status to the community. I wondered if mine showed.

About half the mummy-like figures had cavernous eyes. Others were turned away, disappearing down a long passageway into the rock. Standing with my children, the Great Gallery appeared to be three-dimensional, a portal to the underworld, a slickrock door to the nether regions, Abbey's gateway between worlds.

I remembered our last quarrel over the right to an end. At that time, I believed the rim above the abyss of death had a very sharp edge and that it was possible to regret having stepped over it while on the way down. Now I am not so sure; within that line there appears to be a great deal of space.

Colin, Laurel, Lisa, and I walked away from the awesome panel of the dead and down into the canyon bottom. A mosaic of brick-red mud cracks marked a recently dried pool. I dug into my day pack, beyond the .357 pistol, and pulled out the turkey vulture feather I'd picked up at Ed's grave and stuck it in the mud near a sprig of Indian paintbrush.

As my own culture provides little in the way of ceremony, I continue to borrow and invent my own. I've shared this reverence with my children since they were tiny, having raised them perhaps too much as peers, hoping the deep respect for all life will endure in our blood. I trembled with exuberance because I imagined myself entirely fulfilled.

We turned back downstream. The shadows fell toward sunset. High above, a buzzard floated on the late afternoon thermal. I wondered what he saw, this bird reincarnation of old Ed, watching this ideal nuclear unit of domesticity, the appearance of perfect family, that actuarial 1.8 children, as potentially happy as anyone should ever get.

The vulture circled, looking down one more time at the tiny family walking down a single sacred canyon of the Colorado Plateau, a landscape of second chances.

We drop off the unnamed pass, down over the unstable scree, scrambling to the grassy bottom of Hidden Valley, into the late afternoon sunlight now slicing between precipitous buttresses north of Dhaulagiri. I hit the valley almost running, eager to explore this wild place and see what kind of animals live here. The remote habitat is especially suitable for blue sheep, and if the sheep are here, the snow leopards will be, too. A couple of gentle kilometers down the broad valley, a little sedge-covered knoll rises next to the tiny creek; it will be a good spot to camp.

I pitch my tent on a bench a couple of hundred yards away from and above my companions—out of sight. The altitude of the pass we traversed today was at least equal to the highest elevation I have ever climbed. I feel high in spirits, too, happy to be alive in this wild place, complete in the day. I strip off my clothes and walk naked in the gentle breeze off the mountain, the rare sunlight of the monsoon season raining down on me. A horned lark picks dung flies off yak manure. I flip yak chips over to dry the underside in the sun, yak dung being the only available fuel up here. Four white Egyptian vultures soar above and a swarm of Himalayan doves passes down the creek. A flock of Tibetan snow finches bursts over the ridge and alights upon the open soil among buttercups, asters, ice plants, and other succulents. Just at dusk, a great lammergeier, carrion eagle of the dead—the feathered instrument of Tibetan "air burial"—glides over my camp, turning gracefully against the snowfields on Dhaulagiri.

During the night the fog ebbs and flows up the valley bottom like a diurnal tide, twice rising to a level just below my tent site, engulfing my friends camped below. I sleep. A big cat (a snow leopard?) moves on the boundaries of my dream. About two in the morning I wake to a violent round of my chronic cough and, in my sluggishness, I indulge it a bit. After five minutes of spasmodic coughing, I lie back down and try to sleep. A few minutes later I notice a gurgling in my belly progressively followed by a deeper rumbling lower down in my bowels. I go outside and try to resist the urge to vomit. I have a brief but virulent bout of the runs. What comes out is pure red blood. I try to calmly assess the situation but another gush of caustic hot blood hits my stomach and I gag. The purging is repeated. I monitor the damage: three, maybe four units of blood, maybe two liters lost in all. It's hard to tell; lots of blood. I am bleeding from inside my esophagus. Sobered but light-headed, I lie back down. My stomach feels better; maybe the ruptured blood vessel in my throat has stopped bleeding.

In the west, a white light intensifies beyond anything I can imagine or explain. It isn't coming from my companions far below in the fog and, anyway, this intense light is much too bright to be from a flashlight. Inside my tent, the yellow dome top is lit white as a lightning strike but this luminosity lasts much longer than lightning.

My puzzlement about the light diminishes; it is merely there. I lose track of time. Clearly, with no illusions, I try to concentrate on what is happening to me. My body feels light, as if it is about to float.

Soon, it is daylight. I get up and go outside to check the evidence: the hemorrhaging from my throat has slowed to a leak. I am weak, anemic, hypoxic but not yet in a condition of acute hemorrhagic shock. I can still walk some. But if I blow or dislodge the clot in my throat and bleed again, it will be all over; I will die in this valley.

The first ray of sunlight illuminates an icefall on the high shoulder of Dhaulagiri. Despite my condition, I can't imagine a more spectacular place. In the valley, all is in shadow. A ribbon of ground fog snakes down the creek bottom and disappears into the gorge below. The herd of eight wild yaks has grazed up valley. The fog drifts in and out of the draw below me where Dennis, Alan, and the three Sherpas are sleeping. I look down on their ghostly tents, barely visible then vanishing in the fog, which swirls and pours over the bench.

I decide to let my companions slumber on. There is no point in sounding an alarm since nothing can be done; the clot in my throat will hold and the bleeding will stop or it will not. I dimly reason that I should go for a walk. I want it to be a good one.

I gather up a few items, take the last codeine tablet, grab my old fire-lookout binoculars, and start down the valley. The birds are especially active this morning. Horned larks perch on the tundra and, along with a rufous-tailed thrush and several seed-eating mountain finches, pick insects off yak dung. High above the valley wall, lost in a cloud, an eagle screams. A pair of ravens and red-billed choughs cruise over, checking out the camp. The sun creeps down the slope until the valley is bathed in sunlight. The wet bottom and alluvial fans of the valley are a mosaic of dwarf willow and thin grasses; I can smell the sun on the willows. The far slope of slatelike talus reflects the morning with a blinding metallic light. A reef of metamorphic rock juts out into the valley.

I pick my way through a boulder field of quartz-feldspar gneiss decorated with iridescent green and buckskin-colored lichen. Under one such boulder tiny purple Mycenae mushrooms sprout. I get down on my hands and knees for a closer examination; the damp earth under the rock smells like red Bordeaux wine from the Graves District. I see more mushrooms; conical caps of Panaeolus with close brown gills growing out of yak dung. I mechanically pinch the base of the mushroom stalk for a blue-staining reaction indicating the presence of psilocybin—one of the "magic mushrooms." Maybe I'll eat a handful and see the face of God. But there is no blue stain. No matter, I've already seen Her.

I struggle to embrace all the beauty the world holds; it is almost too much. Up ahead I can see animal trails in the steep scree at the edge of the valley; the sheep are here. A mile north of camp, the miniature creek tumbles along through little gullies and pockets of morainal boulders. I am too weak to go any farther. I climb up on one of the little summits for a last look around. I take two steps and freeze; two hundred feet away a dozen or more Himalayan blue sheep are staring at me. These are a species of animal I have not seen before. They are all females and juveniles including a single tiny lamb—the only one. I know these primitive sheep, which are thought to be a common ancestor of both sheep and goats, rut late in the fall, but I am otherwise ignorant of their reproductive biology. I stand motionless for two or three minutes. The blue sheep resume grazing on the clumps of coarse dry grass. I slowly drop to one knee and ease my binoculars up to my eyes. Kneeling is the wrong move—maybe too snow leopard-like—and the sheep pick up on it. I count eighteen animals bounding away through a knee-high field of brown boulders. One ewe remains behind staring at me for another three minutes then slowly lopes away to join the herd now down the valley and out of sight.

A wave of infirmity shudders through me. I stumble down to the creek, lie down, splash water on my face, then roll over and dry in the morning sun. I am not sure I can make it back to camp. The irony is not lost on me that I am dying in precisely the same way Abbey did. I manage a thin grin. I feel I am outside of my body, watching the crumpled figure sprawled out along the creek bank. I am probably bleeding again. I wipe my ass, checking for blood, as I did Ed's two hours before he died.

"I can't do it," Abbey had said.

"That's what I'm here for," I explained.

Maybe that's what it comes down to, this final humility, the acceptance and service, preparation for the big trip, all shrouded in wretched comedy.

Ever since Ed's death, I thought I was just walking off the chaff of my life, mending, gearing up for more vitality. Now this. But the preparation was, is, the same.

The black tar of my stool is backed up by fresh blood. I am leaking again. I am walking around, as Abbey pointed out, under sentence of death, like everyone else living with a "terminal disease such as life."

Like father, like son.

8 BLACK BEACH

Then it was late summer. Before the kids had to go back to school, I wanted to take a last trip, some place special; with hope we would be able to manage a family idyll. Old fishing buddy Mike was trying out the outer coast of Vancouver Island in British Columbia for king salmon, a remote camp out on the edge of Barkley Sound, among the Broken Group island chain. He drew up a map and told me how to find it.

I drove up with Lisa, Laurel, and Colin, towing a drift boat called the Green Queen. We crossed the international border and picked up the Nanaimo ferry in Vancouver. Lisa's younger brother, Eric, who made his living working as a movie grip, joined us. We headed west through a landscape of clear-cuts to Port Alberne, then threaded back south on logging roads until we hit the sound.

It was a primitive campground, apparently maintained by a logging company as a PR perk to the few people who lived in the region, near the end of a little-used logging road that went nowhere. The camp was unimproved, though there was an outhouse. There were a dozen or so vehicles plus some old trailers; these people came here to fish for king salmon, definitely a working-class camp, the people neither especially friendly nor nosy. A few kayakers bound for the Broken Group archipelago embarked here. The only officials who ever came by were Royal Mounted Police who patrolled by boat and stopped by every week or two to check on things. Otherwise, you were on your own. Totally. Small trailers, campers, and a few aging recreational vehicles were clustered tightly together along a strip of black beach adjacent to the launching ramp. A quarter mile west, alone on a point of land bordered by a creek and a back channel of the sea, sat a single tent. That would be Mike.

We pitched our family tent nearby, at the end of a tidal flat running up a small creek. Eric moved his sleeping bag into

Mike's tent. At least we'd be off by ourselves, away from the other vehicular campers who all needed the boat ramp to launch their big outboard salmon boats. We launched the Green Queen in the creek next to us. The place didn't seem that bad; bald eagles perched in the hemlock tree at the mouth of the creek, clams and oysters abounded, and the fishing was great.

Days passed. Mike was a dedicated fisherman who didn't do much else during his limited vacation time. He would go out at daybreak for salmon, then return and sleep for a while. Eric and I would usually join his excursions, and sometimes Lisa and the children would go along, too.

One afternoon, after a storm, Laurel and I took the Green Queen out into the gently rolling ocean to check on our crab pots. Ours was the only rowboat anywhere around, and my little girl and I took turns rowing, stopping to catch greenling and quillback rockfish on jigs, until we spotted the crab pot floats. The storm had blown them a half mile past the eel grass and brackish creek mouth water that crabs liked. It was a lovely day. We turned back toward camp as the sun set. On the shoreline a black bear came out and started nosing in the oyster bed, gnawing oysters off the rocks. Laurel and I laughed at the little bear. When we arrived at our camp, I jumped out and towed the boat up the tidal channel running up the creek so Laurel wouldn't have to get her feet muddy. Later, Lisa would tell what a beautiful picture it was: father and daughter rowing in on a calm ocean, the sun setting behind. But not now. Now there was trouble.

Eric met Laurel and I at the creek. Our camp was only fifty feet away. My brother-in-law was grim and to the point. Mike had come back alone from fishing and had accepted drinks from two Canadian men camped next to the boat launch. The Canadians, a logger and a highway patrolman, were already drunk. Mike helped them finish a bottle of rum and then invited them over to our camp for beer. Mike had gotten so drunk he had fallen off his folding chair. He finally crawled into his tent and passed out. The two men continued drinking at our camp and had alternated between hitting on Lisa and—the alcoholic flip side—trying to pick a fight. It was all A or B, Eric said, fuck or fight. The danger to Lisa was greater; actually it was a little worse than just hitting on her, he admitted.

My brother-in-law Eric was neither large nor unlucky enough to own the questionable heritage of violent experience. The only time I knew of that he had seen some potentially rough action was a decade ago in West Yellowstone when the locals mistook me and my fly-fishing friends for Hell's Angels in the Stagecoach Bar and thought their claptrap little town was being invaded. Goliath, the tallest and hairiest of our group, instructed Eric to turn the cue stick around and use the heavy end like a baseball bat. But nothing happened back then. Now, it looked like a very bad scene was coming down. Eric had filled his pockets with rocks, big ones.

Lisa had a look on her face I think I had seen before but wasn't sure what it meant. It might have been some kind of exasperated anxiety, a here-we-go-again, the worst of alcoholic nightmares. All I could think was how much I loved them all and how sorry I was I had brought them to this place. But, for now, I considered myself alone in this ridiculously lowbrow but dangerous drama; Eric and Lisa might help me later on.

The logger was tall, lean and muscular; the cop a stocky little banty rooster with a puffed-out chest, smashed on Canadian whiskey and unable to speak, but ready to fight. Both were probably more than a match for me in a fair fight. I avoided making eye contact and kept up a mindless banter with Eric, who lingered nearby, and with Lisa, who had spirited the kids away into the cab of the pickup and locked the doors. The two inebriated men turned their attention to me. The little rooster only wanted to fight now. The cop was drunker and crazier, but I considered the logger more dangerous. The logger wanted Lisa and Colin, then me; he slurred his words but was terrifyingly insistent and still mobile. He'd be the one.

With Lisa and the kids close by but out of sight, the logger and cop decided the altercation was because "they weren't welcome at my camp," and they pushed this button every minute or so with insane intensity. The banty rooster would suddenly lurch over with his fist cocked and stick his red face an inch from my nose. I'd quickly turn and say something about cooking dinner. He did this repeatedly.

I kept babbling about how I had to build up the fire and first feed the kids. It was nearly dark by now, and I knew they wouldn't go away by themselves until they got what they wanted. I kept returning to the truck, randomly grabbing pots, food, and secreting messages to Lisa who had the kids hiding behind the back seat. When the two Canadians weren't watching, I stuck my Bowie knife into the side of my belt, hidden by the heavy Patagonia jacket. By now they followed me everywhere, only a step or two behind. I was almost jogging in little circles to avoid the inevitable showdown. On the next trip to the truck I put a canister of capsicum bear mace in my jacket pocket. Eric got their attention for a second, and I took the duct tape off the safety on the pepper spray, still making small talk about feeding the kids. But none of these defensive weapons would make any difference if the Canadians ever got their hands on me; in fact, they would make it worse, far worse.

This couldn't go on much longer; it was just a matter of when. Only my constant moving away had precluded the fight up to now. But I had to face that once I was unconscious or out of the way, there was no knowing what they would do to Lisa, Colin, and Laurel. The two men would break into the cab of the pickup and take them. There would be no help. The Mounties had stopped by only the day before and wouldn't be back for another week. If these men got their hands on me, it would be all over. Even if I fought them off, they had guns back in their camper and they'd be back.

Lying in the swamp next to the campfire was an old rusted truck axle. I had spotted it among the ferns while pretending to take a leak with the drunk cop pressed up against my back, humping my ass, hoping for a retaliatory fistfight. The axle probably weighed a hundred pounds. I could roll it to my boat. I knew what I had to do. My pulse slowed and my blood pressure stabilized. It was getting dark fast. The tide was in. The cop lurched at me again, the logger close behind. Just a minute, I said, I need to rearrange the fire. I picked up the Army surplus entrenching tool lying next to the fire. I needed to rearrange the coals. After a minute, I unscrewed the folding blade and moved it 90 degrees so that it was at a right angle to the shovel handle. I screwed the blade firmly in place. The rooster jumped in front of me again, his hot breath against my chin. I quickly peeled away, neither looking at the two men nor allowing eye contact even when they were in my face. They were too hot, eager, and overconfident in the security of their little "Deliverance"-style backwater to think anything of the shovel.

By now it was dark. It was show or go. What I had to do was put them both out quick. I figured to go for the logger first. The cop was plastered, mean, and berserk. Once I'd slammed his partner with the butt of the entrenching tool, the cop would come blindly charging in. I didn't think the rooster would fight any harder or smarter no matter what I did to his buddy; it would just be an excuse to fight and he'd be too fucked up to discern my deadly desperation. I planned to take my first shot at the logger just after the point of no return had been reached. I might have to wait until his head was turned, just to make sure, then pop him with the shovel, put him down, and deliver a second shot to make sure he stayed down. I'd figured I'd hit him with the butt of the trench shovel first, just behind the ear, then, if I had to, turn the tool around and drive the point of the blade into his skull.

I had already taken off the safety on the capsicum spray. It would be ready by the time I took on the logger. The cop was drunk enough that I could get to him before he grabbed me. The instant the logger was out, I'd run at the cop with the pepper spray blasting, blinding him, spraying him as much as necessary until I could get close enough to hit him with the entrenching tool, being very careful to keep out of reach. I didn't dare take any chances; I was prepared to hammer the sharpened point of the shovel through a thin area of his skull cap. I was afraid of what these guys would do if they ever got away. They had rifles I was sure. It would escalate into murder. Once I started the chain of events, I could never go back.

In my mind, I covered what I had to do. In the dark, I'd drag the unconscious bodies off behind the tent down into the tidal flat. Once I had them within the high tide mark, I could deliver the coup de grace, if necessary. They would bleed out onto the flat, and the rising tide would wash the blood away. Then I'd slide them over the mud into the tidal channel. Eric would have to help me with the rusted truck axle. We'd load it into the boat. I'd pull the corpses into the channel until the water was waist deep or so. Then I'd bring the rowing dory around. Since it would be dark no one would see. I'd tie the two bodies to the stern of the drift boat and row out into the sound as far as I could in the dark. In the boat was enough nylon rope to tie the arms, legs, necks, and torsos of both bodies to the axle. The ballast of the two bodies was much less than the weight of the axle though it wouldn't be once the two corpses bloated up. They'd buoy up. To preclude distention, I probably should open the bellies with the Bowie knife before pushing the axle over the side. I was hoping I could pivot the axle on one end and roll it over the stern without ripping an attention-grabbing hole in the side of the boat. The crabs would chew through the rope in a few weeks and the bodies would float up but by that time we would be long gone and out of the country.

I went over every detail, allowing no stray considerations to cloud my plan or soften my resolve.

Looking at the ground and clutching the Bowie knife behind my back, I made a last faint plea to the two Canadians: "Why don't you guys just come back tomorrow, it's kinda late tonight."

It was the final appeal. Miraculously, they left us, went back to their camper, and passed out. No one had been killed or maimed. The crisis, it appeared, was over.

Lisa said she thought that I "handled the situation well." But somehow I could not respond. The psychological framing of that particular predicament revealed the heart of my mental illness. I was a true whacko, a real crazy. The incident went way beyond my bar fighting. The shade of deadly violence in my life couldn't be shared. This sort of thing had transpired before, but now became a major fork in the marriage and would eventually sink it. We were no longer living in the same world. In the world I lived in people got killed; sometimes you had to do the killing. I didn't want to disclose that. The same kind of crappy dice throw that had isolated me from my peers after the Tet Offensive was now keeping me from the people I loved and needed most. Why did it all have to be a battleground? Why couldn't my wild and domestic lives marry and be at peace?

Old voices from the bunkers and trenches were again crying out: Don't leave us behind, come join us. The hideous solidarity of the dead was at these times probably more important than my marriage. I wanted to serve and love my children, yet this second calling could not be reconciled with what I called everyday life. After the messy chores of combat, you wanted to wash up a little bit before you played with the kids. Sometimes it took months of scouring isolation to cleanse the blood from your hands.

Ed would have understood this perversion. He saw it when he met the young soldier just returned from Vietnam who, despite his scars, had somehow clung to the elements of his humanity throughout war, who loved the wilderness and who wanted to use the skills of the former to serve the cause of the wild. From the skeleton of this man, Ed had created the fictional Hayduke. The trouble was that, unlike Hayduke, the real man was not content to stay out in the cold; he wanted to cross back over into the human realm. Warriors, however necessary, are not fit company for society. They have trouble entering ordinary life. Purification ceremonies were indispensable.

Standing on Black Beach, I felt far away, feeling like I had back in the desert after burying Ed, still heading down that passageway into the underworld, walking with Ed into death. I thought about war.

9 PETER PIPER

The war went on too long and I never got that second chance. She said I'd already had that opportunity twelve years previous, fucked it up, and that was that. Lisa decided she wanted a divorce: "I don't want you controlling my life anymore," an angry voice crying out, and in a heartbeat, that part of my life was over.

The absolute and sudden end of my marriage was a shock and surprise to myself and the children. In my insular density, I had imagined things were getting better. But my wife wouldn't even discuss cause or reconciliation except to inform the counselor with adamant certainty that my combat disability "should be 100%." I would have done anything to hang in there because of the kids, the family, to whose ideal I clung with unrealistic fealty. But she was right about the marriage. It was shit and had been a sleeping travesty for years. I'd had my clues so I couldn't play flat dumb.

I recall a haze of feelings: depressed, but not hopeless; rejected but not in an important way; cut loose at middle age and angry but not to the bone; loving toward the kids and trying to be decent though this would lead me to walking away from everyone for a while, hurt at giving up my home and possessions. This is freeing but only in the way Aldo Leopold's thousand freedoms were worthless without a blank spot on the map. In the hypertensive weeks of weeping that followed announcement of the divorce, I lost my father, the man I loved most in life, to an aneurysm that suddenly ruptured after forty-five years of dormancy.

I sat at a plastic table in a Peter Piper Pizza joint back in the American Southwest. I had been sitting there for an hour, scribbling some notes and sipping on non-alcoholic beer, waiting on the boys: Colin Stone Peacock and Benjamin Cartwright Abbey who were, despite the three-year difference in age, good friends.

The boys, in the game room, were in no hurry; the return circuit of one of the Skeet ball machines was on an acid trip and Colin and Ben were taking advantage of the endless supply of free balls. Each twenty-point ball got you a ticket and every three tickets would buy a lollipop or key chain. For five tickets you could get an eraser or parachute person. Ben had both pockets full of lollipops and erasers, and Colin was working on a bag of parachute people.

I looked out at the Arizona sky through the harsh glare of the plate glass windows and felt strange, the distant bits of reality hard to hang onto. Maybe I should take a trip: my simplistic solution to everything when my days are wildly out of balance. Especially with more war lying on the horizon. Go down to the Sierra Madre and hang out with Tarahumara Indians.

I was trying to concentrate on the positive lessons of recent years because the last thing I wanted to admit was that the shipwreck of my marriage, subsequent separation from my children, and the death of my father had devastated me, leaving me purposeless and lost. This posture might have been as empty as pride but any old kind of journey beat sitting around.

A true mentor who knows the trail would help. Ed, who was divorced three times, could be my imaginary counselor. Ten years ago, he told me that as you get older, life gets better. "After a while, maybe after fifty," he said, "you make more money. You can afford to take girls out."

High up in the sky, a blizzard of colored objects slowly spiraled on the breeze. I was looking at what might be a dispersed flock of scissor-tailed flycatchers, except that I had been watching when the dust devil hit the Fed Ex drop box located across a busy street. Someone had left the lid off the supply bin and the desert whirlwind sucked out all the paper products—the envelopes, the Fed Ex Pacs and Letters. I watched this spiffy blue and white packaging, like the scissortail with a touch of pink on the sides, spilling out of the great funnel of rising, clockwise rotating air, now floating down like gaudy giant snowflakes over an area larger than a city block.

A Fed Ex Pac dropped into the Peter Piper parking lot. Debris floated above the buildings, suspended in the void of colliding air currents.

^^^

The next day, my soon-to-be ex-wife invited me over to my ex-home at a specific time to pick up some things. I poked about for camping gear inside the storage shed in the backyard until Lisa called down saying there was something I should see in the house. I walked through the back door. The front door was ajar. My wife was hurrying the children down the hallway to the back bedroom. I caught the tight, determined expression of fear on her face as she pushed Laurel and Colin into the room, shouting at them to hurry and just get in there. I heard the door close. The lock clicked shut. The children now had a frail protective barrier from their father. I could imagine them all cowering frightfully in the corner of the bedroom.

I heard a noise outside and looked out. A burley deputy sheriff stepped from behind the palo verde tree and stepped to the door. His hands were hidden behind his back. He reached out with his left arm and handed me papers, telling me I was served and that he was sure sorry to have to do this to me.

I started the pickup and drove away, toward the old barrio section of downtown Tucson. The literary agent of my friend Jim Harrison had kindly loaned me the use of his empty adobe house. I parked the truck, retrieved my 9 mm Berretta, stepped into the house, carefully checked it out, and locked the door behind me (the owner had once encountered, hiding behind the bedroom door, a naked intruder who he finally subdued with the stock of a .22 rifle).

The old adobe had a tile floor under a high ceiling and was sparsely furnished. I poured a whiskey and sat on the floor with my back to the wall. After a while, I thought I heard something heavy on the roof. I went into the fenced-in backyard for a look. It was dark. Someone was running down the alley. I climbed over a high wooden gate and began to chase the sound down the alley.

The next thing I remember is finding myself naked, squatting in the corner of a room with a cocked automatic pistol in my hand. I was cold and sweating at the same time. The scene was familiar. I thought I might be at Bato, in Quang Ngai Province, at the house of the Montagnard commander of the Province's Regional Forces. It was Tet again.

It had been a suicide mission. The command at Danang had ordered one of the nine Americans on my A-team to cross the treacherous river and spend the night as liaison with the Regional/Provincial Forces. Provincial Forces here were ethnic Vietnamese; Regional were all Hre Montagnard. Because they expected to get overrun this very night, late in the Tet Offensive of 1968, all the Provincial troops, along with the Vietnamese District Chief, had deserted, taking refuge in the coastal cities. In general, the Vietnamese abhorred the Montagnards. The Vietnamese troops occupied the only defensive compound; the Montagnard Provincial troops had only the commander's (Dinh Kha) house with barbwire strung around it. By now, main force VC and NVA troops were streaming back from the cities, overrunning all government outposts on their way back to the central highlands. Dinh Kha's villa had virtually no chance of surviving the night.

I volunteered for this dead-end job. The rotation dictated the assignment go to Cool Hand Luke, a black sergeant from Chicago, who had a family; but of the nine Americans, I had the best chance. Still thin odds, however, I knew the language, had won the loyalty of these tribal troops in the last ten months, and was the most experienced local combat veteran at the Bato camp. Also, by that time, worn down by more than a year of uninterrupted war, I really didn't give a shit; I doubted I would be killed (I was so far gone I thought I might be a Ghost Dancer) but wasn't much concerned either way.

Someone drove me across the river on a deuce and a half just at dark, and I walked up the only street of Bato to Dinh Kha's house. Kha met me at the barb wire gate with his huge mastiff. A much-decorated soldier, a hero who had fought the Vietminh all the way through Dien Bien Phu, the commander's betel-juice-stained gold teeth flashed a grim greeting. He walked me around the perimeter of the compound and pointed out a trench running down toward the river. Once the enemy sappers blasted through the perimeter all thirty of us would be on our own. I'd brought my own wire cutters, knowing what to expect: cut the wire and run for it. The commander brought me back to the front porch of the house where I could string up a hammock and watch the night. There wasn't much to say; Dinh Kha had been fighting for thirty years, and I had been in country less than a year and a half.

I climbed into my hammock, wearing my web gear with my survival stuff and leaned an M-16 where I could reach it. The hand grenades on the belt were uncomfortable. I checked in with the A-team across the river no one would cross at night, then set the PRC-6 radio nearby. I got out my Colt .45 automatic and chambered a round.

I lay there with the automatic in my hand across my chest for a long time. It was past midnight on a dark night. Finally, I heard the distant barking of village dogs in the outlying hamlets somewhere within the two-mile "safe zone." The barks were joined by voices and screams punctuated with rifle fire. The growing din of the advancing VC and NVA troops formed a semicircle pinning us to the river. An orange glow crept out of the horizons until I could see the flames from four hamlets. Three of these "resettlement" villages were Montagnard, the fourth, Vietnamese. They were burning everything. Dinh Kha joined me on the porch. I radioed the A-camp; I had to stand by as they were ordering up air support. There was nothing to do but wait till daylight. Stray rounds were cracking nearby so I squatted in the concrete corner clutching the .45 pistol.

It was that night the VC and NVA herded up villagers from the burning hamlets and drove them across the river. My A-camp called in gunships with miniguns that hosed down the entire scene. While I squatted impotently by in the corner, a bystander on Dinh Kha's porch, more than 180 civilians were caught in the crossfire. Enemy troops ran by on the street twenty meters away. We held our fire. They never came for us.

I was shivering. I now knew I was in Tucson, not Vietnam. I grabbed a blanket, rolled over onto the floor, and fell asleep.

^^^

In the seasons that followed my divorce, I stumbled about the American West as the nomad I had always been. The death of my father was, for me, still shrouded in the poisonous ambience of the break up. This I would walk off. It was not lost on me that, up until recently, my luck had been very good. Nonetheless, I slipped a bit on the psychological peripheries of my wanderings.

It was hard to acknowledge that my behavior may have shifted beyond my control, but I could not deny there had already been serious consequences. It was a slippery slope, an area of my life I'm never quite comfortable sharing, but of course, it's right there every day.

Shards of memory were etched in a notebook: At night, I drove out into the desert, loaded pistol under the seat, drink in hand, traveling the dirt tracks for hours until the alcohol pushed me toward troubled sleep. My dreams were all nightmares during which armed enemies hunted me while I fumbled bullets, unable to run or fly away. Three hours of restless slumber was my nightly average. An unshakable sadness shrouded entire days.

Depression stripped me of my sense of humor and reduced the volume of my voice by half. During those weeks, I met an invisible friend with whom I spoke Vietnamese on four different occasions. Once, I woke up with my hands on my partner's neck, not knowing where I was. I dissembled then, pretending it was something else. But it wasn't.

I craved a crack of insight into this darkness. I turned back to Ed's writings, seeking utility, and then to other sources.

Abbey had views on war and warriors, which he had invested in George Washington Hayduke, who made his fictional appearance in 1975, five years before official recognition of the syndrome known as post traumatic stress disorder (PTSD). Ed nailed the PTSD with visionary accuracy and sketched the character of Hayduke with the insight that George's great anger resulted from witnessing injustice—such as events in Vietnam—and that this rage could be turned into a positive weapon, especially in the war against industrial desecration of the wilderness.

Though Hayduke didn't look like he was especially fragile or appear to be the sort of guy who would agonize over matters of the spirit, the source of that anger had everything to do with soul; his great anger and damaged soul were in fact polar worlds in balance.

My war was neither fiction nor an unfortunate slice of life from which one skips cleanly away. There remains the unavoidable price to be paid for discovering that all things are indeed permitted. Beyond this door lie dread as well as knowledge, partially compensated by the closing of other pathways, which could have led to the kind of existence you might, when younger, have imagined lay in store for you. That part of life is hacked off like a finger or an ear. You mourn the loss but never really try to get it back.

The metamorphosis out of mid-American idealism into my second life was forced by the confrontation of evil in the world. Evil can be glimpsed in the malice of a stranger's glare or in the germ of a poisonous thought tucked away in a corner of our own cerebrum. It's all over television and on the streets. You don't need Bosnia or Rwanda when your neighbor's child parades morning bruises and he's beating the dog—the suffering of innocents always close to the core.

The final installment arrived when I saw the photographs of the My Lai massacre in *LIFE Magazine*. I think it was 1969. I was in Tucson, at the house of Ned Spicer, the eminent anthropologist, a generous and humane man who had taken me into his home. There were several pages of photographs. As I turned each page, layers of denial peeled off my brain.

I had known such atrocity prowled the earth. In Vietnam, individual monstrous events, the murder and rape of civilians, happened every day. Massacres of non-combatants, little My Lai's, were common. But the scale of the My Lai massacre made me literally tremble. My soul shuddered. That image of slaughtered babies lying bloody in the ditch was seared across my consciousness forever.

I was nearby when hundreds of men, women, and children were massacred by American troops on March 16, 1968, in the district of Son My, Quang Ngai Province, South Vietnam. It was my last day in the field, the boonies as they were called, on my second tour at the A-camp of Bato, in Quang Ngai Province, a little more than thirty miles south-southwest of My Lai. Later that morning I boarded my last helicopter for the ride up the coast to Danang. We flew directly over the hamlet of My Lai. I had no idea, of course, that at that very moment American GI's were systematically executing as many as a half of a thousand unarmed civilians as we soared over.

Not that any of this was significant beyond sealing a tiny part of my personal stake in the massacre. Except that this was my war, my home province in Vietnam, and what happened in My Lai somehow became my emotional responsibility. This irrational leap led to an obsession about whether I could have done something about it.

What sickened and drew me to the slaughter at My Lai was the knowledge that more than a hundred American troops had been on the scene, many more saw or knew what was going down, and so very few (with the notable exception of WO Thompson) spoke out or acted to try to stop the killing. A thousand times, I dreamed or imagined myself at My Lai and wondered exactly what I would have done; I couldn't quit reliving this fantasy. I believed then, want to believe now, that I would have done everything in my power to make the soldiers who were killing humans, many of them children, like cattle or pigs, stop—or die trying.

Of course, the fantasies were impotent. Instead, I went on stumbling through a disordered life with a renewed vigilance aimed at precluding more My Lai's, hardly a practical readjustment tactic. New wars could trigger these ghosts. You never really left the killing zone, and perhaps, I never will.

Another problem of my particular kind of war is that you were supposed to die, but I didn't. This failure somehow permeates one's ability to live a normal life. Some old soldiers I know have escaped the isolation of survivorship by maintaining ties with other military men, either by staying close to former comrades, by living near Army posts like the wild knot—a very mixed blessing—of ex-Special Forces retirees near Fort Bragg, or by joining military organizations or other professional groups. But the ex-Green Beret medic living alone in the mountain cabin may find his dead twin barring the door to the rest of his life. After all, it is an accident he is alive, a miracle he ever had a wife and house. Being a father somehow comes easier. But the old trooper is otherwise without insight.

Thirty-some years after leaving Vietnam, like thousands of other veterans, I remain hypersensitive to war. The discussion of butchery in the remote world is never quite safely compartmentalized; it's no dark abstract or journey up a river of esoteric horror. Armed mobs and confrontations may jolt us, waking phantoms, shades that re-emerge during certain times of stress or crises that trigger rampant recall of the otherwise selective memory of war, failures of recollection that shield and insulate the fragility of the soul.

Scott Carrier, a friend of mine who works for National Public Radio, spent the summer of 1992 interviewing schizophrenics for a medical survey. When asked what they had in common, he said they seemed to possess weak or damaged souls. Whether they were born that way, or had been some how smothered, he didn't know. Scott thought that the impaired soul—in the case of these frail humans—and the lack of a sense of nature were the same. Whereas native and other peoples maintained intimate relations with rocks, plants, and animals, schizophrenics wandered without significant attachments to their physical surroundings.

A notion of hell would be to not live in a physical world. Abbey once said: "A man without passion would be like a body without a soul. Or even more grotesque, like a soul without a body." Hayduke's wounded soul drove an angry fist and such passion, Abbey understood, emerged from a relationship with the natural world and all its inhabitants. Hope and redemption lives in that wildness.

^^^

Three years into my wanderings in the Western mountains and deserts, a government rating decision arrived: "Evaluation of post-traumatic stress disorder is increased to 100 percent, on a permanent basis." The determination of "Total and Permanent" was made within the Veterans Affairs, a process that included a number of doctors, hearing officers, and appeal boards. Some of the symptoms make the subject sound like a real spit-dribbler, and I'm certain my hearing officer was disappointed I didn't appear to be an exact match. But I continued to deny aspects of the diagnosis and to hide others. There was a frail logic in this: I refused to let what seemed to me an unavoidable and common consequence of war to mortally disfigure the core of my being. At the same time, the government was stating quite clearly that I was totally whacko and forever unsuited to operate within what they called civilization.

As I had no intention of succumbing to helplessness, I swallowed the fact of total social and industrial impairment. We lived in two different worlds: the so-called mainstream, as represented by the U.S. Department of Veterans Affairs, and my own, culturally skewed toward the wild but, I thought, valid enough slice of reality. The VA had labeled me a misfit, and I considered the society it represented a pathological nightmare to which no one should consider readjusting. The message was that I was now the outsider, isolated if not unique. I accepted, and accept, their appraisal.

I believed the conventional interpretation of this disability—chronic adaptive disorder—misleading. Those few story nuggets my uncles, who fought in WWII, shared with me have informed and stayed with me throughout the years. There is great need for the knowledge and the journey of modern men of war. And, as every warrior should know, within the traumatic memory of war and violence, which the soldier often initially avoids, there resides an invitation for change. Here is an opportunity to cross back over from the domain of the shaman to the human world with the story of the journey and the knowledge it contains.

"Total and Permanent Impairment" could be seen as a modern, metaphorical equivalent of bestowing "death eyes," which would have been a great honor in shamanistic culture. Disabled vets might wear the invisible tattooing as a mark of distinction, a ritual scarification denoting your changed status, and as a warning to others that you have traveled beyond.

Whether acquired through war or some other trial and peril, the idea of "death eyes" means to see with complete objectivity, like the eye of nature, to see not good or evil but what is there prior to any judgment. Such refined perception is needed today to confront the reality of our world—a terrible reality from which we would like to turn away, or spruce up, pretend it's not happening.

The notion of "death eyes" or "seeing with the eyes of death," though largely uncharted territory in our culture, survives from the preliterate as myth. Terry Tempest Williams and my sister Phyllis guided me to a Sumerian tale, *Descent of the Goddess.* (My friend delivered the narrative along with this bedrock quandary: "Until men embrace their own feminine nature, there will be no peace.") Recorded on clay tablets in the third millennium B.C., these poems tells of the descent, and subsequent return, of the goddess of heaven and earth into the underworld to encounter her dark "sister." This version is the oldest known of many such myths. All lie solidly in the realm of the feminine—no accident—and I hesitated at first to force a comparison with men at war. But the imagery was compelling.

War is also the story of initiation. Soldiers often return with death eyes; these may be the eyes of depression, to which all life looks dead, or the eyes of anger and withdrawal. Like the initial return of the goddess, it can be demonic and wrathful. Though ultimately this explosive negativity stands for life, her return from the underground first unfolds very much like the classic PTSD symptoms of the returning Vietnam veteran. This is not, I submit, a condition addressed by anger-management classes. The warrior has faced fear and an adversary too powerful. The soul flees. The instinct, at the onset, is to hide out from life until the opportunity arises to be reborn into more merciful borderlands. Meanwhile, the damaged spirit descends back into its painful refuge of the underworld.

In war, as in myth, no mortal can look at the naked face of reality and escape unscathed, innocence becomes impossible. It remains for men to complete this passage; the dark wisdom is absolutely relevant, the perfect time for all warriors, men as well as women, to return—if they can endure it—with the story of their journey.

Under the shadow of Dhaulagiri, in the tundra bottom of the 16,000-foot-high glacial valley, I ponder my predicament: I've bled out about two quarts of blood from the tear inside my throat and it's still leaking. It seems I may not be going home; there is only the present but there is work to be done. I dig out my notebook and scratch out a short but adequate will, then a note to my children telling them I am sorry to have broken my promise to them about coming back, that I know they will be sad, but that I don't want them to be sad forever.

"Larry, I salute you. Laurel, Colin, I am sorry. I love you all." I scratch out this final good-bye to the immediate members of my clan.

The truth is, although I am a bit faint from the loss of blood and the high, thin atmosphere, I feel good today. What's left of my rational mind argues that I'll probably not get out of here. I again find myself able to wonder at the very remote odds, yet appropriate fate, of passing as old Ed did.

I pack my notebook away and stand. I black out for a second and stumble into the creek; the glacial water in my boot shocks me awake and, I look around the valley: Blue sheep trails are everywhere. The snow leopards must be here. If I only had a week, I might spot one.

I start back up the creek toward Alan, Dennis, and the Sherpas. A flush of warmth sweeps up my legs. I labor up the beautiful valley.

I stumble back into our camp below Dhaulagiri. I sit down with my companions and explain that I am unwell. I feel self-conscious, talking with a slightly painful embarrassment, as if the family dog had been run over in the middle of a traffic jam and you are reluctant to share your private grief with a crowd. Alan talks of simply getting me down, maybe to Jomsom at eight thousand feet, in order to fix things up. His is a climber's world of logistics, and it is perfectly understandable that he doesn't quite see that this is only a stranger's death—beyond his or anyone's control. I explain that I have begun to bleed again and that if the bleeding continues I will not make it out, adding that I am out of cough-suppressing codeine tablets. I stop short of telling them where and how to stack the rocks because the young Sherpas seem uncomfortable. I smile, feeling warm-hearted toward them all. There can be no evacuation by helicopter—as if we could find one—Alan says, because choppers cannot fly or land in this thin air. I will have to walk out. Dropping down into the gorge and following the boulder-filled drainage out will be impossible. We will have to climb over the pass. I nod, thinking we necessarily travel alone now. But somehow Dennis comprehends the quietness of it all, the finality and resignation.

Sitting with the men, I sink contently into the present, with friends if not family, in this wild valley looking up into a slice of blue sky over the greatest range of mountains on earth. I remember back to my boyhood during the frigid winter of 1963, in Algonquin Provincial Park in Ontario, when I became hypothermic and wanted to lie down in the snow and go to sleep and never get up again. Now it is much the same. I need never to rise again. The climb out over the 17,230-foot saddle seems both unnecessary and impossible. The pass looms quite beyond my imagined range of movement: I think I will never get there. My head rests against a rock. The immaculate snowfields on Dhaulagiri smile back through a hole in the sky. I dream somewhere short of sleep. I can stay here in this valley, if I must, on this little grass-covered knoll. There is no irony now.

I rise from my bier of sedge and step off the grassy knoll four steps. Lying on the heather is the white feather of a buzzard. I bend over and pick it up, telling Dennis: "I'm going to need a bit of luck."

Dennis takes the beaded Arapaho Indian medicine bundle off his neck and places it over my head without comment. Dennis tells Al we will go straight up the big ravine, a distinctive landmark, so we all can find each other on the broad pass. We start off, leaving Al behind with the Sherpas to organize the breaking of camp and to follow behind. I trudge up the gentle valley never imagining for a moment that I might make it over the pass.

We strike off to the east, toward the steep scree below the pass now fifteen hundred feet above us. The others will pack out my gear. I carry no pack, no extra weight. Still, it is all I can do to inch up the slope. I place one foot in front of another then repeat the gesture. I stagger with dizziness and start blacking out. I squat in the rocks with my head between my knees. Below, the wildly spinning valley returns to a still frame. A raven croaks by. The fog is closing in. I mumble something to Dennis about hoping his knife is sharp. He thinks I am asking him to chop up my body for the birds, but I am attempting the frailest of jokes.

Actually, I don't know what I mean. We continue. Halfway up we are engulfed in fog. Dennis tries to push me straight up the ravine, but I am weak, and I don't think I can make it up. I contour south. We lose each other in the fog. The roar of distant avalanches surrounds us.

Dennis finds me in the fog and tells me we are lost. We are too far south. It will be dark in a couple of hours. We must make the pass. To be caught out on the vertical scree at 17,000 feet will be too much exposure. We are also nearly out of drinking water, which I sip to quiet my cough that may dislodge the clot in my throat and start the bleeding again.

One pitch leads to another, one slope to another, and before the sun disappears behind Dhaulagiri, I step up and see the summit of the pass.

Dennis grabs my arm and pushes me to the northeast. The fog breaks and we find Al sitting on a rock, whistling.

"Hey mates, where've you been?" Al asks. The Sherpas emerge from below the horizon and catch up with us. We assess our supply of drinking water: less than two quarts for six men.

The broad pass leads east toward the foot trail that descends nine thousand feet to the settlements in the valley. I clench the white buzzard feather in my fist like a flightless Dumbo fearing to soar. If I could make it down, maybe I could catch a plane in Jomsom and fly to a hospital where I might be transfused and then—just like Ed Abbey's grim prognosis—expect the actuarial six months of additional life. Even a single month looks like a deal from here. I could see my children and maybe take a last walk.

A great lammergeier soars just above the level of the pass. I try to joke again about "air burial," whereby, in this land of limited wood, the body is chopped into pieces and disposed of by carrion birds as opposed to the tough job of a ground burial up here. The young Sherpa men are not amused. They are right; anywhere would beat being buried up here. The digging is hard and Nepal too distant for my kids to visit.

Where I get planted is important to me. I was never serious about wanting to be cremated or fed to the buzzards Tibetan sky-burial style. I felt cheated when Gage committed suicide and was cremated and scattered before I got the news; I wanted somewhere I could go to visit him. Later when Ed Abbey died, I was of course on hand to see to the logistics. Abbey wanted to nourish a plant, a cactus, or a tree. We should all be so lucky.

We start down. From the pass, it doesn't look so late. We might have an hour, maybe more, of daylight. We must find water.

I am faint, hypoxemic. I stagger. Dennis props me up. Dennis asks Al if they should rope me to someone. Al says no, "if he falls, he falls." Al is back in the mechanics of the professional climber. It's up to me if I live, he says. I lose track of time. We have descended below 17,000 feet. Soon it is night. We stumble on in the dark. Dennis is pushing me on now. Al is lost. We are off the trail. The ridge we are descending is very narrow and falls off treacherously on both sides. We are lost. Very lost.

My cough is back. There is no water to suppress it. I hack and rasp my way through the darkness. I feel the trickle of blood from my throat hit my stomach. I gag and double over, coughing. Shit. We are far off the footpath now. Yaks have made the dim trail we are following. It is very steep.

Dennis hears me, and I tell him that I have begun to bleed again. I must have water. Dennis wonders if we can send a man down to find water and bring some back. Al says no. We move on. The steep yak trail levels out. We stand on a tiny flat. Should we go on in the dark or stay the night here without water? We don't know because we are lost.

"Goddamn it, Dennis," I say, "just make a decision."

10 AFTER THE WAR

The next spring, on the anniversary of burying Ed Abbey (and also the anniversary of the My Lai massacre, my Day of the Dead), I took a trip into the heart of the Sierra Madres—one of a series of great trips with the man who had become my favorite traveling companion into the wilder regions of Northern Mexico. The time was also toward the closing stages of one of our recent wars, which spurred our restlessness to disappear into the rugged barranca country of steep canyons, homeland of the Tarahumara Indians. Kim, who had lived there, was my guide. We wanted some distance from all the flag-waving.

There had been recent trouble in the Tarahumara; Indian land was again being encroached upon and usurped by Mexican nationals who were moving into the sierras to cut timber and plant plots of poppies and marijuana. The intrusion of the dope trade into this remote region had raised the stakes all around, and automatic weapons were not uncommon amid a traditional culture that until the last few decades resided largely in the Stone Age.

We drove east out of Tucson and south up into the gently rolling Arizona tableland that is the northern extension of the great cordillera of the Sierra Madre, passing through agave-studded grasslands and oak-timbered benches rising toward Mexico. I asked Kim about the junk littering the dashboard of his pickup truck, and he identified a pre-Columbian frog figurine, the severed paw of a small mountain lion, a hawk's claw, and three little flags—Iraqi, Serbian, and Afghanistani, which Kim had bought at the Maps & Flags Store—now wound with red yarn, branches of sagebrush, and an owl feather into a kind of shaman's bundle.

Kim was long and powerful with quick moves, surprisingly feline and agile for a big man, just under 200 pounds. In his late 40s, he was still one of the most physically gifted men I have ever known. Before he became the 82nd Airborne's heavyweight champion, Kim had never boxed. Between the Army and the present, he had drifted along the border of Mexico and Arizona, moving easily among the mestizo and Indian people, like a great solitary eagle of the barrancas, the effortless master of language and culture.

I was an ex-soldier who shared Kim's uneasiness with the national glee about our one-sided military victories. Nobody begrudged the troops their homecomings. It was the tacit assumption that war could be as painless as a video game that we could not abide. Kim only avoided Vietnam because he was an Olympic hopeful who fought his way to a boxing championship at Fort Bragg, North Carolina. My own Special Forces unit was also based at Fort Bragg and I didn't avoid the war at all. Both our outfits, the 82nd Airborne and the Green Berets, figured prominently in the Iraqi wars, Somalia and Afghanistan, and we had watched the action unfold with considerable interest. What had driven us down here was the absence of dialogue about the price of war, the unburied dead, civilians caught in the cross-fire, the refugees, the incinerated crews in destroyed vehicles.

Just ahead was the small town of Agua Prieta, a lawless, brutal border town of drug smuggling and mass murderers; seven bodies had been found on a ranch just east of town, five of them stuffed down a well. A couple of the corpses showed signs of torture; fingers had been cut off.

Agua Prieta is the end of the road for much of the dope grown in tiny plots down south. What begins as a petty cash crop in the barranca country escalates rapidly as it accumulates and passes through middlemen along feral corridors into the violent greed and quick riches of the border towns. Life gets cheap.

This is a Catholic country, I thought, its paths are stained with blood of the victims of God's avengers: the dictators, presidents, popes, and generals. This is the pragmatic verity, as opposed to a state-sanctioned capital punishment, which is not law. After all, Jesus was an executed criminal and who wants to believe in a God who metes out torture for torture and pain for pain?

We passed into Mexico, without incident. Kim had spent considerable time down here. He studied the traditions of Native American peoples, spoke their languages and, when culture permitted, participated in their ceremonies. One of the reasons I valued Kim's companionship was because he was not a modern American; he was as expatriate as anyone with a driver's license could ever get. In another earlier time, his cosmology would have placed him firmly in the realm of the shaman.

This was not to say he was always a pleasant animal to hang out with. He never quite relaxed; he always seemed to be working. On the other hand, travel with Kim was never recreation, you were always in the real world, living your own life, and what happened in it was important.

Below the U.S. border, the Mother Mountains of the West rise into the zone of timber, and this forest continues along the Sonoran-Chihuahua state line all the way south into Durango. We drove through Mennonite farming country to Cuauhtemoc, then turned south, following the railroad tracks south to Creel. Smoke from kilns and pulp mills filled the mountain air with the pungency of pine and a hint of juniper. Creel itself is a rough-hewn town hugging the railroad. Flatcars carried American Winnebagos and other recreational vehicles chained to the beds, waiting for the next engine to Los Mochis. On the streets of Creel were other Americans: tall white girls with long hair avoiding eye contact with other gringos, maintaining their sense of exotic isolation. Another knot of gringos with light backpacks and trekking garb, perhaps part of a guided group headed for Barranca del Cobre, waited outside the train depot.

Although the Sierra Tarahumara is a small part of the Sierra Madre Occidental, this homeland of about 20,000 square miles contains three huge canyon systems—all deeper than the Grand Canyon of Arizona—emptying westward onto the plains of Sinaloa: the great barrancas of the Rio Urique, Rio Batopilas, and the Rio Verde.

Tarahumara people (Raramuri in their own tongue, meaning "foot runners") number perhaps 45,000. In their mountain vastness where terrain is steep and roads few, the Tarahumara have found the most efficient means of travel is on foot; they walk and run across the vast distances that separate them and that have historically insulated them from the efforts of the Spanish and others to civilize them.

Spanish contact with the Tarahumara began in 1607 with efforts to relocate the Indians; Jesuits urged the natives to resettle around the missions. Then, in 1631, a rich silver deposit was struck at Parral and laborers were needed. The Spanish hunted down "wild" Tarahumara and forced them to labor in the mines. Tarahumara children were kidnapped under the pretense of taking them to mission schools and brought up as servants. Spanish settlers appropriated the best lands for farming. Tensions arose and a Tarahumaran by the name of Teporame emerged as an opposition leader.

In 1650, rebellion broke. The Jesuit missionary at Villa de Aguilar, near Papigochic, was killed with extreme hostility, as evidenced by the degree of mutilation of the body and the crucifixion of the missionary's soldier protector. The fighting fanned out and a state of siege, punctuated by three revolts, reigned until 1652, when Teporame was executed. A relative period of peace lasted to 1690 when a new rebellion broke out.

In 1696 the missionaries heard what they thought were rumors of revolt, and sent for the Spanish commander, Captain Retana, from Parral to provoke battle. Although the Tarahumara did not want to fight, Retana still rounded up sixty Indians at random, killed all of them and cut off thirty Tarahumara heads that were impaled on poles lining the road from Cocomorachic to Yepomera. Fighting broke out again and Retana graced the vicinity of Sisoguichic with thirty more heads on the ends of sticks. Great savagery characterized this last rebellion. Entire bands of Indians refused to surrender; for the Tarahumara, resistance to the Spanish became a way of life, and they accepted death willingly, preferring to die in battle than to submit.

The Spanish military conquest was effectively complete. Another silver rush began in 1709 and the Tarahumara who chose to resist assimilation now retreated westward into the rugged barrancas of the Sierra Madres. European depredation of Tarahumara people and appropriation of their land went on for two centuries; the 1825 Law of Colonization opened up all uncultivated public land to Mexican colonization. This process continued well into the twentieth century. The result was further withdrawal of the Indians into the rugged canyons and mesas, and a deep-rooted distrust of all things European.

These cycles of conquest were repeated throughout the New World. In the case of the northern Mexican tribes, such as the Tarahumara and Seri, Spanish colonialists saw themselves as civilized people dispensing civilization to barbarians and savages for the good of all. In practice, what these occupational forces from the land of the Inquisition doled out was something far less than civilized, and often much more than barbaric. The Indians were treated like "animals." There is nothing new about this, of course. It is our story: herding up the villagers of Bassasorichi or Pitic, Wounded Knee or My Lai, driving them into a ditch and mowing them down or otherwise dispatching them like pigs.

One reason people like General Rentana tended to treat the Indians like animals was precisely because the colonial Spanish had no relationships of any kind with animals except domestic ones, such as dogs and horses, which they tended to treat brutishly.

Anywhere I walked on my own continent, these little loops of history ran through my head. I'm certain other cultures had their own versions; I just knew my own best. This was the way we wrote our story, the price of conquest, the deadly trail of Manifest Destiny paved in smallpox-laced trading blankets distributed to the

Mandans, spreading rapidly upstream after 1834, decimating the Missouri River tribes; pacification in Southeast Asia, war in Asia and the Middle East; more treachery here in the Sierra Madre. You walk through this land with the past in your backpack.

Traveling through the Sierra Madre Occidental, the Mother Mountains of the West, on the eve of another war, I thought about the Tarahumara warriors and how, in Vietnam, the myth of the gunslinging Western hero swaggering into the frontier sunset had finally died an overdue death. The recent wars saw the enemy exploding and burning as lit on electronic video screens safely distanced from blood-spattered realities. There are no heroes; in the wake of the new, clean, cold killing, the long-distance slaughter of modern push-button warfare, the warrior was gone forever and the butcher home to roost.

South of Creel, toward sunset, the country opened up and we saw the yawning chasms in the earth, the big canyons of the Urique and Batopilas. It took your breath away. Nothing since Tucson had given us any hint of this gigantic, improbable terrain.

In the gray distance, a Mexican black hawk soared on the last thermal of the day and the slow staccato of a Tarahumara drum rolled up the canyons. That night we camped on a high ridge between the barrancas of the Rio Urique and La Bufa. Kim still owned a house and an orchard down there, where he briefly settled after a decade of fighting to save sea turtles. Like others who live with bold and far-ranging movements, he carries no interest whatsoever in the notion of adventure but owes the range of his life to simple restlessness and curiosity. In 1972, after his stint in the Army, he crashed his Cessna 172 in the Ecuadorian Andes. He somehow walked out. That same night, he knew that adventuring, as the driving force behind his travels, was inadequate metaphysical fuel to propel a life. A year later, he saw three live green sea turtles in the back of a pickup on their way to the slaughter house near Kino Bay in Sonora, and the die was cast.

Later, Kim became my partner for skimming the hills and canyons of Northern Mexico; his knowledge of the country, consummate linguistic skills, and expertise in the nuances of culture were unparalleled. We took trips into Baja, the Cabeza Prieta, into the Sierra Madres to search for grizzlies and Mexican wolves, jaguars in the island ranges of Chihuahua. He took me in when I separated from my wife and later took care of me after the divorce. He settled part-time in La Bufa, though "settled" in Kim's case was more akin to the last Mexican lobo living among hostile goat ranchers in the colonized Sierra Madres. His closest friend there was a Tarahumara named Ramon, a man I wanted very much to meet.

In the morning we packed up and moved on, dropping down through the chaparral into the barranca of the Rio Batopilas. We jolted down the treacherous road into an unfamiliar forest of big morning-glory and kapok trees studded with organ pipe cactus. At the bottom was a tiny village of a dozen families, each yard flush with the muted blossoms of spring—the village of La Bufa.

Ramon Figueroa was waiting on the road below Kim's house. We gently touched the insides of our fingertips—a handshake in the manner of the Tarahumara. Ramon was a handsome man, even among a people known for their physical beauty. He wore traditional dress, a collared turquoise shirt with long sleeves worn over a loincloth tied over the hips with a colorful woven sash. Ramon claimed to be "around thirty" years of age and, although normally shy and taciturn around strangers, his quick smile made him look much younger.

Two sets of drum beats now rumbled in the canyons. The Tarahumara country itself appeared to have its own cadence, own way of seeing. Perceptions of "reality," of course, had something to do with why we had come down here after the war. We had been escaping a dose of our own consensual reality, fleeing the headlines of the daily news that told us supporting the war effort was more important than what actually happened in the war. Fortunately, then and now, the most ordinary of options provided solace. Our choice—and one cheap-ass, easy way to broaden one's view and prick one's curiosity—was travel, to go somewhere new and different. I had gotten down here on three tanks of gas for Kim's pickup, down into these implausibly rugged barrancas, a light year away from any notion of modern war and among the Tarahumara who, like the Kurds of Iraq or my own Montagnard of Vietnam's highlands, are a tribal mountain people having problems of their own.

The four wheel-drive pickup rocked and groaned along the pitted track south of the town of Guachochi. The road led to the edge of the mesa. Chest-high walls constructed of volcanic boulders lined the roadway. A hint of gray-green lichen attested to the antiquity of these lovely stone walls. Beyond, gaped the enormous gorge, and the narrow, green ribbon below. Kim and Ramon joked about the relative smallness and insignificance of their homeland barranca of La Bufa, and Kim teased Ramon about meeting his new father-in-law down in the barranca of the Verde.

When the jokes died down, Ramon quietly noted he really wasn't ready to look for another wife yet. His wife had died of tuberculosis the previous June. Ramon had only been able to return to work in January and, even now, eight months into his grieving, he found it difficult to carry on.

In the distance, native drummers again beat to drive the spirits of the dead out of the cornfields. The Tarahumara people—who say that the dead plant corn in winter, that a person's soul travels when the body sleeps, and that night is the day of the moon—believed the souls of the dead must be properly dealt with.

On the benches south of the barranca of the Rio Verde are winter homes for the Tarahumara who move up into the pines of Pino Gordo in summertime. Wood smoke billowed from a half dozen locations. The Indians were preparing *tesguino* (weak beer made from corn or agaves) for Holy Week, the time before Easter when fields were prepared for planting, a time of celebrations and *tesguinada* (the occasion of drinking beer) for Christian and pagan Tarahumara alike.

These beer busts are the central event in Tarahumara life, the social grease, an anodyne to the harshness of everyday life. Each adult spends about a hundred days a year preparing, drinking, and sobering up from *tesguino*. Attending one of these events was a serious commitment; you needed to have a couple of days to blow off. The idea of a *tesguinada* is to get a "beautiful intoxication." In spite of the centrality of drinking in Tarahumara social life, there is little alcoholism of our Western variety among them. Private drinking is all but unknown. The notion of rich Indians brewing up a continuous supply of beer for their exclusive use brought peals of laughter from Ramon.

In the evening we camped among pines overlooking the barranca of the Verde. A stiff wind blew out of the west. Without a fire, the night would be cool. I had brought some extra gear for Ramon, a blue pullover and a Patagonia pile jacket. I passed these out and turned in.

By mid-morning, we were ready. Ramon, who was still bundled up in the black pile jacket, remarked that he "felt like a sheep" in its nodular fur. Shouldering our backpacks, we ambled through the last fields, passing stately live oaks and elegant walls of stone. The trail forked and Ramon took the less traveled route that leaped over the rim and fell down a thousand feet in a dozen steep pitches. The three-needle pines of the rim gave way to oaks, then progressively to desert scrub and big cactus forests. At the bottom of the six thousand foot gorge tropical vegetation covered the oldest layers of rock. As we descended into the barranca we left the twenty-first century behind and dropped through time into the world of the Rio Verde and the Stone Age Indians who still lived there. The morning sun had climbed high and beads of sweat rolled down my forehead. I stopped to admire the branching roots of a fig tree caressing the contours of the yellow cliff.

With binoculars we glassed the far side of the barranca. Wood smoke told Ramon that Tarahumara families were out of corn and were roasting agave hearts to make *tesquino.* We crept down for another two hours until we stood on a little finger mesa that was a giant leap above the inner gorge of the Rio Verde—a braid of turquoise pools and white rapids. Our hearts took a leap as we saw that two Mexicans with mules were already taking a break there. We had heard many reports and a few horror stories about the drug trade in this area. Recently, we were told, a botanist had his mules shot dead by dopers here in the Sinforosa.

Though the two mestizo men didn't talk much, they were not wearing pistols and weren't otherwise menacing. They were leading the mules down into the Verde then out south toward Pino Gordo. Through the plastic sacks they were using as saddle bags I could see small packages wrapped in plastic and newspaper and taped crosswise. I avoided staring at their cargo, which we figured to be drugs or money. At any rate they were in the business.

Once we left this well-used trail down into the Rio Verde, we would encounter few people. Yet the barranca country was not wilderness. The Tarahumara, hard-pressed by industrial encroachment, their land expropriated by Mexican nationals, have traveled almost everywhere in these broad, deep canyons. Every suitable flat or bench in the barrancas has been cleared and planted with corn, beans, or squash at one time or another. Some of the rugged, narrow side canyons are wild, and there are a few pockets of relative wildness surrounding isolated buttes and mesas. Elsewhere, the larger wild animals have been hunted off and domestic livestock have penetrated nearly every niche.

^^^

The situation was no surprise; I had known this from Ed Abbey, who had come here in 1978 to see the barrancas and write a story. In particular, it was the piece Ed wrote that drew me down here. His essay, "Sierra Madre," closes with these two sentences:

"The world is wide and beautiful. But almost everywhere, everywhere, the children are dying."

Ed noted that the Tarahumara way of life was being threatened, constricted, "closed in upon by massive road building schemes, by heavy logging in the mountains." Still, the Tarahumara Indians certainly looked at life through a different prism than did the mestizo or Anglo visitor. The nomadic Tarahumara here still practiced slash-and-burn agriculture in the barrancas and subsistence agriculture elsewhere. They lived on the tentative edge of agriculture but somewhere beyond the parameters of hunting and gathering, which no longer provided a total alternative. Their cosmology lingered somewhere in-between.

The Anglo and mestizo perspective lacked the long and sustaining tradition of indigenousness with the land. Ed thought he recognized in this view symptoms of our own cultural ills and a prototype for American population segments. Strung along the northern industrial outposts of America, what we used to call the frontier, are the rootless and unattached of our own, anywhere boomtowns providing trailer sites and big wages. Ed also sensed this estrangement in the American West where groups of angry men talk about taking the land back. The groups are overwhelmingly white males. Loosely, the land-use groups are woven into an apocalyptic network which, especially in the Northern Rockies, slops over seamlessly into county separatists, armed private militias, and the Aryan Brotherhood. Today, the focus of this fraternity is against wolves and grizzly bears. This hostility toward other races of humans, native animals, and the wild land are connected, born of the same antagonistic alienation.

This attitude is nearly opposite that of indigenous peoples, such as the traditional Athapaskans of Alaska or the most remote Tarahumara, who maintain a relationship with the land that is symbiotic and therefore sustainable. Ed saw that the displaced pods of Anglo industrial culture are emblematic of a deeply troubled connection with the natural world a genuine sickness. Abbey went on to say this: "But where, how, did the disease begin? It really does seem to me like a cancer, a tumor on human society. I would say it began when we gave up the traditional hunting and gathering way of life, and made the terrible mistake of settling down to agriculture. Someone said that the plough may have done more damage to human life on the planet than the sword. I'd be inclined to agree."

These attitudes, which have characterized our species since the beginning of time and were only recently misplaced, are also central to individual change; the will to change an individual life today still means to reconnect spiritually and metaphorically with those wild relationships. You could see it all right here in the Sierra Madres. Below, in the barranca of the Rio Verde, the white froth of rapids separating the necklace of placid green pools twinkled an invitation.

^^^

A thousand feet down the trail we came to a flat. Suddenly Ramon and Kim stopped and signaled me forward. Sprawled in the trail, as if carelessly tossed upon the rocks, was the body of a Tarahumara man. We stepped around, just beyond machete range, and checked his breathing. Was he dead? No, but he was in a deep sleep, snoozing off the *tesquino* party of the previous night.

We continued down the steep, rugged foottrail that switchbacked down a near-vertical slope. The temperature dropped slightly in the late afternoon shadows and the crystalline descending notes of canyon wrens accompanied us into the chasm. We dropped down the last steep grade onto the bench. This is easy enough country to travel through on foot if someone shows you the trails and tells you where they go. Strange trees sprouted giant white flowers and cotton balls. The Rio Verde ran cold and deep but not too deep for crossing at the foot of most pools. Two Tarahumara families who had been sitting on the rocks upstream started up the steep trail toward Pino Gordo.

It was getting close to dark and we needed to find a campsite. We worked our way upstream, hopping boulders along the river's edge. The boulder field pinched against a sheer cliff, which we managed to climb over, passing up our packs. Only one pitch of cliff proved un-climbable and that we waded around, holding our backpacks over our heads, waist-deep in the river. Behind us, the Indians hooted and shrieked from the mesa above; they were waving their arms telling us that the trail we wanted was above the cliff, laughing at our pathetic efforts to get upriver. It was too late for us to turn back so we just went on, providing the evening entertainment.

Finally, we rounded a bend, out of sight of the howling Indians. Before us was a beautiful pool, shaded with great oaks and sycamores, with a sandy beach on the far side. We forded the river and threw down our packs. Even Kim was beat. Only Ramon, all iron from the waist down, showed no sign of exhaustion. Across the pool a pair of cinnamon teals rested on a rock in the current. Debris hung in the trees a full twenty feet above the present water level. This would be a poor place to be during heavy rainfall. Just at dusk, a pair of river otters swam out from their den, their lustrous coats curling against the dark surface of the pool. They rolled and frolicked in the current, diving for fish until darkness settled in over the barranca.

We stoked a fire in the rocks and rolled out our bedrolls. The night came alive with jungle voices of frogs and toads, joined just after dark by the yippings of elf owls, keeping me awake until about midnight when the temperature dropped, putting all the cold-and-warm blooded animals to sleep except the owls and Ramon who sat wrapped in his blanket by the fire.

In the morning, the otters again played near the head of the pool. Kim was paying Ramon good commercial wages to act as a guide for this trip. Still, I was unaccustomed to Ramon's wood gathering, dish washing, and water purifying, preferring to do these little things myself. This egalitarian disposition was dented when Ramon could not resist sneaking up on the otter sleeping on a boulder and winging it on the side with a rock.

"He wants to take the otter home," explained Kim as we suddenly became bosses and educators, dispensing the usual lame gringo eco-speak about how you could only kill and skin the otter once but might enjoy seeing it many times. I was less than comfortable in my role, because I was the outsider, but thought it nonetheless correct.

Kim, who lives in the mountain peasant's world as a fish in the river, went on to tell me another animal story, a disturbing parable of cruelty in Tarahumara country, as if to beg the bedrock question plaguing his twenty-year love affair with the disenfranchised of Mexico: Are dominance and the infliction of suffering an inescapable chunk of the social contract? This was, in a way, why ex-Spec 4 Cliffton and ex-Sgt. Peacock were here seeking a clue, an insight into modern war and history.

^^^

I recalled a serious conversation (facilitated by passing around a whiskey bottle) I had with Ed Abbey back in 1973, around a campfire in Aravaipa Canyon about cruelty, war, murder, and history—a story that I now shared with Kim. Ed and I had talked about specific horrific acts and how far we would go to stop it; would we be willing to kill? In defense of family, home, the innocent? It was a tough one. I then confessed to Ed how I almost had to kill another Green Beret, an American noncommissioned officer, in Vietnam. Up until that time, I had never told anyone about this surreal moment in my war life.

This Special Forces intelligence NCO had led a patrol into a bombed out valley twenty miles southwest of Danang in February of 1967. I was the only other American on this routine operation of 25 Civilian Irregular Defense Groups (CIDG) irregulars and a Vietnamese interpreter.

It was my first real combat patrol. By the time I realized what he was doing, the NCO had called in artillery on a bunch of people coming in from a day's work in the rice paddies.

"Mainforce Vietcong maneuvering in the open in squad formations," he said over the radio. They were just a bunch of fucking farmers. We blew them to hell.

During the following six weeks, I watched this guy request nightly "Harassment and Interdiction" howitzer fire on senseless civilian targets in the "Freefire" zone. His mindless irresponsibility led to "friendly fire" casualties. He never did anything to me, so it wasn't quite personal. But this guy caused a lot of innocent people, including many children, to die and, just a few months into Vietnam (I became jaded quickly over there), I decided if I ever got sent out with him alone again on a combat patrol I would have to waste this fucker. It was possible to think like that in such a place if you really didn't buy into any of the patriotic bullshit about the war; for me, by that time, it was just arithmetic. It didn't matter if he was an American or not.

Fortunately, before our operational rotation came around again, I got transferred to another team down in Quang Ngai Province.

My new A-camp was a better place. The war still went on but was somehow cleaner. I trained medics and nurses, built hospitals, and became the most combat-experienced team member during the next ten months.

Just before Tet, a new intelligence NCO showed up on the runway. It was him. Despite my lowly rank, I had enough influence on this team to hold the reins on this motherfucker, to render him relatively harmless. The roulette of patrol rolled around again and it came up me and him. There would be no interpreter because we were short and by this time I spoke Vietnamese well enough not to need one. It would just be me, the intelligence NCO, and twenty handpicked CIDG, mostly Yards, whose trust I had earned, and whom I could count on for loyalty and silence. I had it all set up. The only trouble being that it was one of the rare joint operations with a linkup planned with an American infantry company out of Duc Pho (the same outfit responsible for My Lai).

We set out from the Safe Area heading north into country controlled by the local VC. Though the intelligence NCO had rank, I kept control of the patrol by virtue of the time I had spent with these irregular mercenary soldiers and my knowledge of the land and language. The NCO had picked up a case of dysentery and stopped often to go out into the bushes by himself. I figured one of those times I'd go along for security, just pull the pin on a hand grenade, and come back in by myself claiming a booby trap had done the job. The little people, my CIDG, would know what had gone down but would stick by my story.

The second day out we hooked up with the American infantry company that had been choppered in from Duc Pho. The platoon had a VC prisoner they turned over to us for interrogation. The Americans were burning hootches in a Vietcong controlled village and shooting the pigs and water buffalo. This sickened my people except for the dense intelligence NCO who joined his countrymen in the fun. I watched him walk into a flooded field where four water buffalo stood. He walked within thirty meters of one buffalo and opened up with his M16 on semi. The buffalo turned and, despite his wounds, charged his ass. My fellow Green Beret was about to get impaled on the curved horns of the water buffalo. The NCO fell into the paddy. The big animal was a couple meters away and still coming. This all happened fast. There was probably a smile on my face because of the good karma of a charging water buffalo that was about to render my plan to kill the NCO unnecessary.

At the last second I brought up my CAR15 and shot the buffalo through the front shoulder. He dropped dead four feet from the prostrate NCO. I was stunned. I didn't know why I did it; it was the only water buffalo I ever killed. The dumbass, murderous NCO was lying in the mud, his face ghostly white from the near-death experience with the buffalo and from his case of the runs. I walked over to him and told him to get his pathetic ass on the chopper and get medevaced back to camp. Otherwise, he'd never get back alive. I didn't say why. Maybe he knew. I just wanted him out of there.

The truth was something had happened to me. I felt real bad about the water buffalo. The NCO hadn't been worth saving but he wasn't worth killing either. I just didn't want to have to look at him anymore. After that, somehow the war ended for me; I didn't want to kill anything. My shooting days were over.

That afternoon we took charge of the VC prisoner and started back through a jungle trail that led back to the A-camp. The prisoner was from the hamlet the Americans were burning. My troops knew who he was; he was no more and no less VC than anyone else in the Vietcong controlled village. The local war was still like that out here in the remote countryside in early 1968.

Dinh Ut, the Montagnard platoon leader, and I took the Vietnamese prisoner off by ourselves, off the ridgetop, and down into the high elephant grass. I took off his blindfold and told him in Vietnamese to turn around; I cut the cord that bound his wrist with my K-bar. I told him it would work out OK. That this was just to cover everybody's ass. Maybe he believed me. At least, there was no fear on his face. I handed Dinh Ut my Car15 and took the Colt .45 out of the holster on my web belt. I checked the chamber and pointed the automatic in the air. I squeezed a single round off and replaced the pistol in my belt. "Di ve nha," I said. Go home. I turned and followed Ut back up the hill.

Back in Aravaipa, I had said to Abbey that I had no wisdom but I nevertheless believed it was our cruelty—the individual inhuman act—that keeps the freight of murder, genocide, and torture hurtling through the night. The converse is that the individual act of restraint, grace, and compassion, with its attendant affirmation of the value of an individual life, can begin a revolution.

That night in the barranca of the Rio Verde, Kim wasn't sure. But, me, I still believed it.

The revolution could start right here.

^^^

We spent two slow days trying to get upriver. We encountered a Tarahumara man who hurried away without a word and a pair of Mexican cowboys who told Kim they had come down there to collect four goats from a Tarahumara family. They then gave Kim a piece of rock with fine calcite crystals presumably showing the proximity of silver, since we gringos were no doubt down here for gold and silver and would of course want to look at their mine. The taller cowboy's ferret eyes darted about for opportunity as he talked, flashing bad teeth. The shorter mestizo looked at the ground, fingering his machete and rocking nervously on his new shoes.

After they left, Ramon told stories. Years before in the town of Batopilas, he was carrying a huge load of dry fodder on his shoulder and "mestizos set it on fire." Ramon laughed. He said mestizos who sold *tesguino* to the Tarahumara often put human shit in it, so the Indians only bought from Mexicans who would not decline the offer of a drink of their own beer. Mormons baptized Ramon when he was two years old in the Batopilas River. "They almost drowned me," he remembered, "it was cold and deep." So that was the end of his religion, the formal kind anyway. And though he didn't believe in hell, he thought there was a devil who had a bitchy wife and that their many offspring were mestizos.

By late afternoon of our third day in the barranca, we found ourselves cornered by sheer cliffs and deep water and, having no easy alternative, we hesitantly made camp close to the mestizo encampment. At dusk, the two cowboys boldly crossed the river to talk, making both Kim and Ramon nervous. Ramon said that since the mestizos had new shoes they must be in the drug business. Even Kim was uneasy now that the Mexicans knew where we were camped. Just at dark, we moved camp again and deposited our gear on a tiny beach littered with cow and goat shit.

The three of us had planned to separate in the morning, with Kim and Ramon climbing up to Pino Gordo and me exploring up the Verde. "The coyotes will eat you," smiled Ramon, meaning the cowboys with new shoes. "They are probably sharpening their machetes," he added with a broad grin. But Kim turned serious. "We can't split up," he said, "the stuff we're carrying is worth more than they make in a year. These people have nothing to lose."

I watched the fish rising for insects at the tail of a little rapids. Two hummingbird-sized moths bombed the pool, laying their eggs in the quiet waters.

At the bottom of the deepest canyon on the continent, I sharpened my Bowie knife and prepared for the night with my two comrades. Quite late, the barking of Indian dogs awakened me. I noticed Ramon sitting by the fire, watching over us, waiting for cutthroats who might steal through the dark. I experienced a moment of vulnerability in a land where life was cheap and people had nothing to lose.

We moved off at first light, crossing the Rio Verde where it boiled up between two big rocks. I slipped on an algae-coated boulder just upstream and was swept into the rocks, one of which I bear-hugged, throwing my weight and Kelty pack over the top of it. In the middle of the river, I moved on, stepping once into a waist-deep hole and soaking my sleeping bag. I avoided further mishap by leaning on my cane staff. A dipper bobbed on a riverside boulder. In the damp sands on the far side of the river, there was a cat track the size of an ocelot's.

We had been out only four days but Ramon had grown more and more homesick for his children. Although he was close to home and in country almost identical to that in which he had grown up, he was inconsolable, and by our fifth day in the Rio Verde country, our friend became a lost soul. We camped upriver among gigantic igneous boulders by a swift channel. I kindled a fire out of the wind while Ramon sat staring into the side of the Buick-sized rock at the reflected flames as if the stone were a window into the other world. Kim asked if Ramon would like to climb up toward Pino Gordo the next morning. He replied that he would dream on it to see. Ramon sees all his future, and that of his children, in his dreams.

I went off alone and made a small camp, the muffled roar of the rapids lulling me to sleep. That night the female jaguar came to me in dream again, the big yellow cat prowling the banks of the Rio Verde, circling my sleeping bag. The feline dominated the "sexual woman;" I wanted her but I also feared her.

Waking, I kindled a fire in the sand next to my sleeping bag. The jaguar still prowled the shadow of my dream. I tried to think about the dream while it still lingered. I thought the dream was about children. Did I want to have another child? What was this? My marriage was dead and gone. Maybe the jaguar dreams were also about alcohol; it had been weeks since my last drink. These big cats only visited my dreams during periods of sobriety. A couple of glasses of wine a night would make them disappear. In the dream, the jaguar told me to quit drinking so we could continue our dialogue.

The cool air settling along the Rio Verde from the rim five thousand feet above sobered me. By now, I was wide-awake. Like Ramon, I listened to my dreams. They were harbingers of change: my life in transition—the painful metamorphosis, insects molting and lizards shedding their skins, marriage outgrowing its partners.

At dawn, the songs of flocks of Cassin's kingbirds rang from the sycamore trees followed by the shrill barking of tiny elf owls calling from their holes in the ghostly white-scaled trees. Ramon had no dreams to report, no surprise since he had sat up all night by the fire. He said this was because he was watching out for us, making certain no one sneaked up in the night with a machete in hand. Ramon was also concerned with the souls of the dead who move in the night. These, he said, might be bats or other winged creatures.

We packed up and moved downstream, crossing the river above a logjam. The river crossing wasn't nearly as tricky as it had been the day before. Sycamores marked the junction of the side canyon. Buried under a stack of logs washed down the canyon by floods, was a "violin log"—a log of the scarce conifer the Indians used for making violins. This was the most animated Ramon had been in five days, as if the wood reminded him of music, and he needed music.

He languished for his children. The three oldest were off at government boarding school, which was mandatory for Tarahumara children to attend. Sometimes he saw them on weekends. His three-year-old lived with a sister at La Mesa above Batopilas. When we told him we would be heading back to La Bufa in two days, he seemed cheerier.

We broke for a bit of lunch. I lit a fire and prepared soup. Across the river sat a vermillion flycatcher—Kim's favorite bird. Ramon told us about his infant daughter who had died two months after the passing of his wife. The child had been taken in by his sister-in-law and had died during a *tesguinada*, he didn't know exactly how. His relatives hadn't given him an accounting yet. Someone might have gotten drunk and fallen on the baby or dropped it in a fire. It had happened, the dark side of *tesguino.*

We headed for our old camp at the otter pool. Mats of native cane grew along the high-water beach. It was late afternoon. Kim decided to explore downstream. Ramon sat atop a boulder carving a flute from a section of cane. I watched the small clouds of insects lit by shafts of sunlight filtering through the green sycamore leaves. He carved on into evening, until we heard four perfect notes from the head of the channel drifting across the Rio Verde. Again, the flute blew four undiluted tones into the fading light. Unable to bear this purity, I retreated downstream, climbed up a great boulder, and sat overlooking the long green pool, watching the chubs rising to caddis flies and suckers flashing alongside dark rocks.

Finally, Ramon fell asleep. Each night he had sat by the campfire, tossing logs, tending the blaze until daybreak, guarding us all. Within the underworld of the Tarahumara, it was at night that the spirits of the dead wandered about. Women have four souls, unlike men who have but three. His wife and daughter moved in the day of the moon. I wanted him to sleep in a world where children didn't die.

I sat motionless on the rock for almost an hour looking at the fish, hoping the otters would reappear. Far overhead, a dark raptor stooped and plummeted toward violet-green swallows. I brought my field glasses up and watched a peregrine falcon pull out of her dive, joined by her smaller mate, then returned my attention to the river. A small iridescent green bird flew up the pool into a live oak. Suddenly, a hidden hawk hopped off a rock and nailed the "parrotlet." I watched the black hawk pull strips of flesh off the green bird still anchored under his left talon.

Green feathers drifted down from the branches. I picked up a primary and carried it to the Rio Verde, placing it on the eddying current. All life, these deadly birds, so precarious and precious. The feather entered the flow and disappeared down the canyon. The souls of the dead were at rest.

In the morning we climbed out of the barranca, reaching the mesa and the pickup by late afternoon. We bought beer in Guachochi, drank, and melted together in the manner of *tesguinada.* I impulsively gave Ramon the handsome turquoise shirt and a matching blue mini-mag flashlight to see him into the night. Ramon insisted on two Polaroids of the two of us, one for each. We smiled together while Kim snapped the Polaroid. I signed Ramon's photo and he signed mine. Ramon disappeared in the darkness of the Sierra Madre Occidental. Before we drove off I glanced at the signature on the picture in the light of my small flashlight. It said: "Ramon Figueroa, a brother."

Again, one last time, I heard the four perfect notes floating across the green pool of the Rio Verde.

The next afternoon, in a mountain pass of the Sierra Tarahumara, Kim and I stopped at the crest of the road between two blunted summits. Kim grabbed the medicine bundle, his memorial to the war dead—the flags, owl feather, and sage wrapped up with red yarn. In the ebbing sunlight he dashed across the road and ran up the side of the mountain, a burst of power and energy, climbing all the way to the crest.

From the pass, I watched him digging a hole where it would face both the rising and setting sun. I gave a little salute. Kim buried the war bundle. Above me, a red-tailed hawk hovered in the stiff breeze, finally gliding into the gathering dusk below.

On the tiny flat atop a narrow ridge below the angular, chiseled goddess of Dhaulagiri, on the lineation traced by a yak trail, Dennis decides to stop for the night. The night is black, and we are out of water. My cough has returned, and I am bleeding again. Dennis has informed me that his blood type O is compatible with my type A and that he will transfuse me. Of course, we need the needles and tubing from below. The Sherpas, especially little Pemba, are afraid I will die, and he is concerned that "I should have time to die." Big Pemba holds the knot of tribesmen together. They are all afraid of traveling in the mountains with death as their client.

Dennis peels off his pack. It goes crunch. A tiny bank of brown snow!

We almost walked right by it. We touch the snow; it is the color of siltstone but still snow. It is possible only Dennis knows what this means: with water I have a chance. It will soothe my throat and give the bleeding a chance to clot over.

I feel too far gone to make sense out of anything. Acceptance reigns. The men take charge and try to melt snow for drinking water. Al's stove won't work but Dennis', functional for the first time on the entire trip, fires right up. The purification filters repeatedly clog from the silty snowmelt. Somebody puts up my tent. Water is boiled. They make sweet Sherpa tea.

Dennis asks if he should stay with me—throw his sleeping bag in my tent. No, I answer, thanks but I would like to be alone. I want to concentrate on what is happening to me.

During the night it rains hard, solving the water problem. Al and Dennis stay up and listen for my cough. They get up in the pounding rain, driven by flailing wind, and rock my tent during the middle of the night. They make certain that all is shipshape and that I am alive. Dennis is not sure I will make it through the night, since I'd already lost so much blood before we found the snow. The men smoke some black hash to keep their spirits up.

At daylight I clear my throat. Dennis and Al hear it and know I am still with them. I stick my head out the tent flap to see a crystalline blue sky. Everything is immaculately white with fresh snow. The sound of avalanches, now falling off the slopes every few minutes in the morning sun, fills the air. Dennis walks over.

"I would like to just sit here a while," I say. "It is so beautiful."

But Al says we have to go and he is right.

Dennis and I go ahead, leaving Al and the Sherpas to break camp again. Soon the faint yak trails converge to form a larger path, which after a couple hours leads to the route by which we climbed up only a week before. It's a simple matter of going downhill now. I think I might reach the valley. With luck, I could see the kids again.

We drop down the footpath four, maybe five thousand feet, we are still far above the valley. By now, I think I can make it to Marfa. It will be a very long day. We pass the high pastures where they were bleeding the yaks on the way up. There are trees now, cedar and five-needle pine.

Our descent has taken us from about sixteen thousand feet to nine thousand with one thousand feet left to go. Dennis is suffering excruciating pain in his quadriceps, an old football injury. I ask witlessly if I can carry his pack, as I have carried nothing since the bleeding began.

"No," he snarls.

We pass rock walls. It can't be far to the village now. I see a big weasel with a lot of yellow on its throat. Below twelve thousand feet, the acacia are in bloom: a pale rose with a flush of scarlet. Stacks of fire-wood outline the rooftops of Tibetan houses. The trail is well used and slippery with coarse alluvium, the glacial outwash that accumu-lates in valley bottoms. We are down. Possibilities swell.

Huge hand-hewn, yak-transported slabs of slate pave the narrow streets of Marfa. Dennis is still in great pain, having descended nearly ten thousand feet in a single day. I am simply grateful to be in the physical world. I feel no concern for my body, beyond the desire for the continued heart beat. We will go to Bhahti's teahouse for the night.

Walking along the cobble and slab streets, I savor the aroma of cooking fires, the fetor of yak, even the smells of human squalor. I hear a tinkle and watch in rapture as a lively horse from Mustang—wearing a beautiful leather saddle, a thick wool blanket woven with snow lion designs, and bells—trots through Marfa.

We arrive at Bhahti's. Al and the three Sherpas arrive at almost the same time. The men are starving. Food is served. I consume nothing but a cup of weak tea. Later, Al buys a bottle of brandy, which is distilled locally from homegrown apples.

I take a tablespoon of brandy and bend my nose to the glass. The alcohol carries the sweet fragrance up my nostrils, and I remember where I last smelled this scent: an abandoned orchard swallowed up in sumac and jack pine on a hillside in northern Michigan, the last place in the country where you could still buy an acre of land for $150. I discourse at length (as Dennis will remind me later, my low-blood memory as dispersed and free spinning as pollen grains) on the distinct olfaction of place, of big cats and bears, of brandies, wine, and wild mushrooms.

Not to be denied, I add distilled water to my tablespoon of apple brandy and have a drink with my friends. I don't want it to be my last.

^^^

The mountain village of Marfa lies wedged against the western bevel of the Kaligandi Valley, a level oasis in the angular, windswept, dusty country. Now in the heart of summer, the fruit trees wear deep apple-green cloaks as we walk up valley to Jomsom. There, we take a room in a teahouse near the tiny airport. The regularly scheduled flights to Pokhara and Katmandu are dependent on morning fog lifting before the catabolic winds pick up and blow near midday making landing too hazardous. The window of opportunity for a plane into Jomsom can be very small. Some days it doesn't open at all.

Al is ill. During the night, he had chills foretelling the onset of fever, which when it arrives feels about 103 degrees Fahrenheit. Al is listless, nauseated, and hurts under his right lower ribs. He tries to smoke a cigarette and says it tastes "like yak shit." As an ex-medic, I tell him he probably has acute hepatitis. I came down with it once myself in Vietnam.

Each day is touch and go. Wealthy German ecotourists, stuck in Jomsom, grow increasingly cranky at the inconvenience and try to charter a helicopter. But there is no helicopter. A Thai Airlines plane has crashed near Katmandu and all Nepal's limited rescue aircraft are focused on this disaster. Planes are scarce. With Al sick and me still living with the possibility of more bleeding, we are anxious to get out. Every morning we watch the fog thin and live in the hope of a flight getting in, for a couple hours, until the winds pick up and we know the opportunity is over for the day.

We sleep, read, and walk the airport. My throat feels lacerated but is perhaps healing. I feel I have my bleeding under control here with unlimited drinking water and codeine pills from the little pharmacy shop. Just take it easy and patiently wait for a ride back to the old US of A, where I'll check into a Veterans Affairs hospital and get diagnosed with the presumed bad news: that I have destroyed my liver with booze and that the bleeding from varices in my throat means I have the exact same lousy prognosis that Ed Abbey lived under during his last years. But that's okay.

Wonder of wonders. An unscheduled plane has been chartered in Pokhara and it's on the way here. We scramble. Al exchanges the tickets. The plane lands. They only have room for two. Dennis and I board the plane. Al will catch the next flight.

The plane lands at Pokhara. Dennis and I stay on board and will next fly to Katmandu. No one, nothing will pry me off this plane, which is life or death and my ticket to my children.

On the way in to Pokhara, we rode the local bus from Katmandu bouncing along a rough road for seven hours through Gorkha

Country, winding along the rugged gorge of the Trisuli River. The condition of my throat requires a gentler trip back from Pokhara.

Back in Katmandu we check in again at the Mustang Holiday Inn, definitely not the spiffy chain of motels back home. Dennis calls the airport; all flights are booked. We are on standby. It could mean several days of waiting.

We walk the streets of the city, hiring bicycle carts when we tire. Riding through the town, we pass a legless beggar. I have seen him before. I stop the bicyclist, get off the cart, and walk back to the man. The man with no legs has a broad face very much like my friend Jim Harrison. I hand him some rubles. We both smile. I bow.

"Namaste."

Every night from the roof of the Mustang Holiday Inn, I listen to the hum of the city and watch the swarm of vultures and black kites descend into the trees, and giant coppery fruit bats leave their inverted roosts and fly out over the city, like the changing of the guard.

Al has seen a doctor and received the limited treatment available for viral hepatitis: avoidance of alcohol and other substances metabolized through the liver, bed rest, dietary and vitamin supplements, and a 5 cc gamma globulin shot in each cheek of his ass (ouch). His eyes are yellow and jaundice grays his ruddy British skin. For now, Katmandu is his home.

Dennis and I walk down to the temples along the river Botmai, tributary of the sacred Ganges, where smoke billows from a funeral pyre of eucalyptus as another Hindu soul is reduced to ashes and transported seaward, and self-appointed local guides scurry for position, like pimps for turf, in this holy place of the dead. The one who has leeched up to Dennis tells us we may take pictures from a terrace thirty yards above the Hindu corpse, whose black toes now curl in the flames. We decline.

The fire crackles and the choking smoke floats downstream over naked children frolicking in the filthy water. Black buzzards soar overhead. I remember burying Abbey and the ten turkey vultures high over the Cabeza Prieta. Far up in the sky, forked-tail kites wheel in the midday thermal, the thunderheads building of a south Asian monsoon. Below the vultures, egrets and ravens crisscross the sky.

Dennis and I leave on Thai Air with a stopover in Bangkok and are then routed through Korea. The jet curves to the south to avoid China. After an hour or so I look down on the Danang Harbor for the first time in a quarter of a century. I was down there during the Tet Offensive in 1968. I see Marble Mountain, another holy place where skirmishes between the American Marines and the local Vietcong were a daily event. Pieces of the lovely rose-banded stone of the mountain were carved into frogs with bulging eyes and countless little Buddhas, which I saw everywhere I traveled in southeast Asia.

Sizemore and I sleep. We wake. Soon we are at the airport in Los Angeles, LAX. We fly, at Dennis' urging, two more hours to Salt Lake City, where Dennis lives, and where I go immediately to the emergency room at the Veterans Affairs Medical Center. The doctors draw blood. I sit as calmly as I've ever sat, awaiting the inevitable diagnosis: Abbey's disease. Life expectancy: with luck, a year.

I carve my priorities in the recesses of my mind: to see my daughter and my son. To take one last solo walk to the Grizzly Hilton.

The emergency room doctor calls me in. He has the laboratory report in his hand.

The blood tests are completed. My liver function tests are within normal limits. My hematocrit is low but otherwise I seem okay. The doctor thinks that only the violent coughing, aggravated by medication and not by liver disease, caused the tear in my throat. He calls the rip a "cricothyroid separation." It may never happen again.

I am speechless. I have no clear thoughts; I cannot respond. I only know he's somehow saying that I get that second chance.

From deep inside, as if down a distant canyon, comes a familiar cranky rumbling voice:

"Don't blow it asshole."

11 BURY MY GENOME AT THE GRIZZLY HILTON

The old path is overgrown with bracken fern and huckleberry brush. I push on up the game trail, following it through the conifer forest with only minor difficulty. No humans have used it since I quit coming here over a decade ago.

It is midmorning, and the leaves are still sopping with dew. Downed timbers from the previous winter's unusually heavy snows crisscross the path like giant matchsticks. I pick my way through, carrying an awkward load of camping gear in an internal frame backpack. Here and there the tracks of moose, deer, and bear affirm the relative ease of using this old trail as opposed to bushwhacking through the dense thickets of alder and devil's club.

I move steadily, stopping to listen and scent the air every five minutes or so—all the old rusty senses are slowly coming back to me now. The trail climbs, not steeply, but steadily. The September day heats up. A trickle of sweat runs down my forehead, and I blink the salt away. Two more miles of easy walking to reach the angular flank of the mountain, where the game trails really begin to climb.

Stopping next to a big fir tree, I dump my pack and look closely at a smooth patch where bark has been rubbed off the tree. This is a bear-rubbing tree; a twist of light guard hair caught up in the pitch tells me a grizzly recently passed this way. I am not alone.

More cautiously, I look around and up through the branches of towering larch and spruce, survivors of the fires that sweep through this area every twenty years or so. The Montana sky is cobalt blue with just a hint of afternoon cumulus beginning to ease in from the west. The needles on one larch tree are turning golden. Above the zone of timber, on the high scrub fields of this tiny mountain range, autumn frosts have already blasted the tundra into a brilliant mosaic of reds and yellows. The wind rustles. I hear distant ravens croaking and, from deeper in the forest, the crystalline, flutelike song of a hermit thrush.

How goddamn lucky I am: this is the place I want most to be on earth, and no one else is crazy enough to come here. A small giggle escapes into a bog of alder and red cedar; I haven't felt such delicious anticipation since I returned from Vietnam in 1968 and saw the Rocky Mountains again. This is freedom; an escape from prison would bring me directly here. If I were told I was going to die in six months, this is the first place I would come.

^^^

After my discharge from the VA Hospital in Salt Lake City, I visited my children and made arrangements for them to come and live with me the following summer in Montana. Then I came here, to the grizzly country in and around Glacier National Park.

I drove here in my pickup, passing through the Tetons and Yellowstone Park, which I had believed I'd never see again, where I had camped for months at a time over three decades. By the time I hit the Flathead River drainage, I was goofy with the undeserved prospect of seeing again the place I had come to call the Grizzly Hilton.

By the railroad tracks near West Glacier, I loaded my new Dana pack with a tent, sleeping bag, binoculars, the usual contingency stuff, and enough emergency food to survive for a few days (I plan on living off huckleberries). I grabbed a few hours sleep, then just before daylight drove up the lonesome road and hid the backpack in the brush near my entry point into the mountains. Turning around, I drove back down and parked the truck where it wouldn't be noticed for a week or so. At dawn, I hiked back up the road, recovered my pack and, waiting until there were no cars, darted across the road and disappeared into the trees.

It is important no one sees me come here. Why? Because this spot is small, vulnerable, theoretically too easy to get to. Yet, for me, it's perhaps the wildest place I know in the lower forty-eight. Roads surround the twenty-square-mile area around the Grizzly Hilton making it a pocket of wildness within a domesticated landscape. And it is the grizzlies who keep it that way: wild and formidable, dangerous, sizzling with an energy now rarely glimpsed on this planet. For this reason, I quit coming here myself over a decade ago; I felt my own presence was beginning to impact this primordial scene.

You don't visit the Grizzly Hilton for the salve of gentle nature, a relief from your real life at the office. Here, you live within the land with all its creatures; you engage with it. You have no choice in this realm but to enter the ancient flow of life. This is not the sort of place to compose a wilderness journal of self-reflection.

Using a suitable branch of lodgepole pine as a balancing staff, I edge along a downed tree lying over a swampy section of the trail. At the edge of the bog, colorful mushrooms litter the forest floor: red *Russula* and the brick caps of three species of *Boletus.* I mentally log the location of edible species for my return trip. Red squirrels chatter in complaint as I pass by. Up ahead, through the branches of big trees, I can see elongated triangles of brilliant color from the scrub fields on the upper flanks of the mountain.

In the shadow of a big tree, a cat-sized brown animal with a bushy tail stares at me. I freeze. The spine of the pine marten undulates muscularly as he darts up a tree. I hear the big weasel's guttural hiss as I pass beneath him.

At the tiny creek that drains the area below the Grizzly Hilton, I turn upstream. The game trail widens; the creek bottom is a heavily used corridor. The stalks of cow parsnip are broken and the bracken fern brown and trampled from the passage of big mammals—bear, moose, and elk. I can smell the smashed vegetation as I push through thickets of mountain alder, relishing its sweet perfume. The country opens into small meadows marking the bottoms of avalanche chutes. Overhead, a golden eagle screams. I stop at a muddy wallow in the game trail checking for tracks.

I bristle as a chill rises to the back of my neck. In the mud is a tapestry of bear tracks, most all of them grizzly, so many that I spend the next ten minutes measuring the lengths and widths in order to sort out individuals: There are no less than three grizzly families in the immediate area, two mothers with a cub of the year, if I read it right, and another sow with two cubs. Two other grizzlies have passed through in the last two days, a big subadult (a younger bear separated from its mother but short of sexual maturity—a teenager) and a huge bear. I put my hand down next to its paw print and find it as dwarfed as my confidence. Trepidation clamps down on my chest like a phony coronary. I know this feeling as a beautiful fear. No other creature on the continent instills this most mnemonic and useful of human dreads: the original shudder. Lions and bears at the mouth of the cave of our genesis. We too once were prey.

More alert, I creep along stopping frequently to listen and sniff the air. It's noon, when grizzlies often bed in these cool thickets along the creek. They drowse heavily, allowing the possibility of walking right up on one. That's how many hikers get mauled in the daytime; people stumble upon sleeping mothers at such close ranges that the sows automatically defend their cubs. No animal is more dangerous than a mother grizzly. More than three-fourths of all injuries inflicted by bears on humans are the result of defensive attacks by female griz with young. You don't want to walk up on a grizzly mom, let her wander too close, or startle her on a day bed.

Though I like to be quiet in the woods, I now cough softly, making just enough noise to forewarn any bears that might be bedded along my route. I smile: I have done this many times.

A pile of fresh bear shit lies in the path, a ten-inch pie of blue and red huckleberries. In the little meadow areas are fresh bear digs; the grizzlies may be digging corms of the wild onion. Though berries constitute the bulk of bear diet at this time of year, they always seek a variety of foods. I cross the creek again and fill my canteens. From now on, I'll be living on the dry ridgetops.

On this last stretch of trail, the yellow and red leaves from false azalea and tall berry brush have been knocked off during the passage of many large animals. The leafless level indicates grizzly shoulders. I trudge up the dim path. The grade is steeper now, and I am carrying ten quarts of water. The two liters of blood cells I lost in Nepal have yet to regenerate—I am a bit faint. I stop every few minutes to gasp or to let the woods stop spinning.

The forest yields to a broad meadow that sweeps across the creek and on up the far slope of the valley as a wide avalanche chute. I give the creek bottom a wide berth. From here on is all prime grizzly habitat. Near the top of the chute, the berries are ripe. With another five hundred feet of altitude, I'll be right in the middle of it. More bear shit litters the ground, berry and grass scats every hundred yards or so; with the exception of ants, these grizzlies are vegetarian this time of year. One especially large pile of poop indicates a correspondingly huge grizzly. I wonder if I know him.

I strike off the trail for good, following a dry creek bed to the abrupt flank of the ridge. I plunge though an opening in the thick tall brush. A tunnel-like bear trail leads straight up the steep hillside. I take it, staggering up the hill with my heavy load, the pack straps biting into my shoulders. I grab hold of stout shrubs and small trees to help pull myself up.

In twenty minutes, I take a break in a tiny opening. I dump my pack and sit down with my field glasses. Across the valley, the crimson patches on the hillsides show the location of berry brush. A brown shape moves in one of these. I bring my binoculars around. A large, chocolate-brown grizzly bear browses on huckleberries.

Jesus Christ, I say to no one, I'm home at last.

To tell the truth, I first came here as a wounded warrior twenty-five years ago for the danger. I didn't know why, beyond that the grizzly was considered the most dangerous animal in North America. For all the pain and horror, war teaches little. Its peril led only to killing and destruction. After Vietnam, I was looking for a new, healthier kind of ordeal.

I remember Laurens Van der Post's return from war to his beloved Africa:

> When I came back to the world, after ten years of war, ten years of death and killing, I found that I could not face society. I felt a strange instinct to go back to the wilderness of Africa. I went to live in the bush, alone. I remember the first evening in the wild, seeing the first Kudu bull as I made camp on the Pafri River. He came out of the river where he had been drinking, sniffing the air between him and me. He threw that lovely head of his back, and I looked at him with a tremendous feeling of relief. I thought "My God, I'm back home! I'm back at the moment when humanity came in, where everything was magical and alive, quivering with a magnetism from the fullness of whoever created it all." And I lived there for four whole weeks and gradually, through the animals, I was led back to my own human self.

After my war, home was the Rocky Mountains. I wasn't looking for grizzlies but found them anyway. What was invaluable was the way the bears dominated the psychic landscape. After Vietnam, nothing less would anchor the attention. The grizzly instilled enforced humility; you were living with a creature of great beauty married to mystery who could chew your ass off anytime it chose.

I stash away my binoculars and re-shoulder the backpack. The big brown grizzly feeds on, far across the valley. I turn away and burrow upward. In ten minutes, the route begins to level out. I reach a gentle saddle in a major ridge running down from the crest of this little mountain range. The brush thins out a bit. Stopping to look around and listen, I hear a big animal moving off to my left. A branch breaks about seventy yards away—most certainly a bear, probably a grizzly. At any rate, he heard me. I stand perfectly still for three more minutes trying to determine which way the bear is headed. A soft woof escapes the thicket. The bear is alarmed but not panicked. The sound fades as the animal moves away, down the far side of the ridge.

I move quickly, leaving the grizzly-frequented saddle, and climb west up the main mountain spur leading to the summit. The huckleberries are ripe here. A well-used elk and bear trail leads steeply up the ridge. I am excited now and don't care if I'm out of breath. Stunted, five-needle pine trees indicate the upper edge of the timber zone. A few more steps and I stand clear.

What a vista! I can see the ridgeline rolling all the way up to the Grizzly Hilton a mile distant. I see the entire drainage I have traversed, open scrub fields sweeping up beyond timberline to the gentle summits—several square miles of prime grizzly habitat. In afternoon light, the color is magnificent: red and yellow slopes punctuated by golden larch and subalpine fir; mountain ash all crimson and heavy with red berries. I break out the binoculars. Sure enough, no less than five grizzlies graze the distant berry fields. Besides the big brown griz, I see a pair of panda-colored subadult bears, probably three years old, and two light brown grizzlies of intermediate size.

The ridge levels out. Taking just enough care not to blunder into a feeding bear, I hurry up the crest. The berries still cling to the red bushes in defiance of early frosts. I pluck a handful at the edge of a tiny open saddle that bifurcates the ridgetop.

I make myself slow down, sitting for a minute and taking deep breaths, less from the exertion of the climb than to prepare psychologically for what awaits me just across the saddle. I want to take my time and savor these last few steps. The place is thick with bears this year.

I edge across the gap in the ridge. I hear heavy movement only a couple of hundred feet away in the brush below. It's a griz. It hasn't heard me and the wind is favorable. The bear is feeding; it isn't going anywhere soon.

A few more steps and I arrive at my old observation point and look down on two tiny alpine basins that abut the central spine of the mountain range. The floors of these basins are open, with only a few small conifers growing in the flats, which themselves are not much bigger than a rounded football field. There is a snowfield left over from the heavy winter and small sedge meadows and a little shallow tarn girded by burnt logs carried down by avalanches. The lake is muddy and streaked with the broad roily trails left by swimming bears, cooling down in the middle of a warm autumn day.

The tinkle of water, then a splash, rings through the mountain amphitheater. The reverberating sound is hard to trace. There. Through my field glasses, a dark brown mother grizzly and her sleek cub play in a corner of the tarn. They spar in the water, attack and chew on each other's necks. Above on the hillside, I catch movement; two blond subadults browse only four hundred feet away. I carefully back up a few feet to the top of the narrow, flat ridge to glass down into the opposite basin. I see no bears but hear one moving below. A minute later a small black adult grizzly emerges from the stunted timber. Far above, near the top of the basin, another medium brown bear browses. I position myself where I can see all seven grizzlies at once. Along with the five in the adjacent drainage, that makes a dozen. It's a very good day.

I don't find such dense concentrations of grizzlies here every year. The local population depends, among other factors, on the regional berry crop; if there's a bumper crop of huckleberries everywhere, the bears don't need to come here. Some seasons, the berries fail completely. In that case, grizzlies visit, find little to eat and move on. This year is, so far, one of the best.

I am never so alive as here, alone, watching waves of grizzlies wash across the ridge on which I stand, sweeping down into the opposite basin. The country feels dynamic, too; the shimmering landscape vibrates mystery and danger. I should have lived this way all my life. We all should have.

Of course, we can't and if we did, the Grizzly Hilton would not exist. It is a privilege and a selfish luxury for me to be in this place, and I know it. I have often thought that if I knew I were soon to die, I'd like to come here. The bears would have a snack, and they could scatter my bones. Of course, I'd ask my children first.

It is mid-afternoon. The weather is good and looks to hold. The mother grizzly and her cub have temporarily disappeared. From time to time, I catch a glimpse of one of the subadults high in the berry fields. The ridge is narrow with steep flanks falling off into basins. The westerly winds normally blow my scent away, and it is rare that the grizzlies below are aware of this intruder.

I prepare myself to watch the late afternoon bear action in the south basin, where I expect the most grizzly activity. A small larch tree clings to the lip of a fifteen-foot cliff that drops off to the south. The tree will break up my silhouette. I carefully position my pack behind the tree, comfortably distant from a small anthill. I dig out my extra jackets and spread them on the ground, picking away small rocks and hollowing out a small depression for a hip hole. I lay on my side, hidden behind the tree, my butt snug in the depression. My head rests suitably on the sleeping bag, which is still tied to the backpack. I want it to be perfect.

Before me lies the entire basin, all of the shallow pond and the small snowfield. I roll over on my back, lying motionless for five minutes listening to the gentle breeze. The deep blue sky is shattered into kaleidoscopic fragments by the larch needles. A sleek slate bird with a long narrow tail blasts across the ridge then wheels a loop at eyeball level. I sit up and flick an ant off my pant leg. The sharp-shinned hawk disappears over the next ridge.

A brown animal moves on the flat below. This huge male grizzly grazes on the sedge meadow. I may know this bear. After twenty minutes of observation, I'm certain. Many years ago, he chewed up my sleeping bag and sweaty tee shirt (everything that smelled intimately of me) while ignoring the tent and other camping gear I had cached high in a tree. He is the alpha male of the grizzly gathering up here—the most dangerous animal I know. I used to call him the "Black Grizzly," though he looks dark chocolate brown in the sunlight. I rejoice at finding my old nemesis again. With the Black Grizzly still roaming the world, I feel my life is complete, certainly less secure, but riveted with fresh complexity. In his early twenties (older than me in bear years), I can't believe he's still alive. It is his, our triumph. He is my Moby Dick bear.

Now, however, beauty takes a back seat to caution; I must be careful around this one. Another grizzly, a small blond mother with a single cub, emerges from the timber headed out onto the open flat. Immediately, she spots the Black Grizzly and freezes. The big bear feeds on, ignoring her. She turns her head from side to side and anxiously chomps her jaws. The sow rears to look around and scent the air. The little cub tries to climb up on her back.

Abruptly, she wheels and races uphill, right toward me, heading for the saddle. The mother and her cub climb rapidly up the ravine halfway to my lookout. Now, only 150 feet away, they look directly at me, then glance back on the flat where the big male grazes, distainful of us all. The two bears cautiously continue up the saddle. They will pass over the ridge no more than forty feet from my larch tree. I get ready to back off the ridge. The grizzly family clearly sees me yet they continue to ascend in my direction. This is unusual behavior for the normally skittish mother who obviously regards the Black Grizzly with far greater respect and wariness than she does this puny human.

The bears skirt through the saddle fifty feet away and disappear into the northerly drainage below. They don't even look at me. I return momentarily to my berth behind the larch tree. I retreat again as the Black Grizzly climbs out of the basin and passes through another gap into the next valley, giving no indication he has noticed me, which of course he probably has (this feigned aloofness is a prerogative of an alpha male grizzly bear). My meditative tranquility surrenders to a mild trembling, a visceral fear that I taste in the back of my throat like an exquisite wine.

The hours pass. Slender shadows of fir trees flee across the flat. The mother grizzly and her dark cub re-emerge from the dense undergrowth. They spar and play like puppies for a few minutes on the flat then return to the berry brush. The sow seems secure in her social status within the rough dominance hierarchy formed by grizzlies wherever they gather.

Suddenly, I am aware the entire basin is in shadow. I must have fallen asleep. There is only an hour of daylight left. I rub my eyes and grab the binoculars. A big adolescent grizzly, maybe a four year old, is sitting in a corner of the little lake. The sow and her cub play on the snow patch fifty feet away. This close grouping of grizzlies is atypical. The cub romps over the hard snow, tries to dig into it, then bites his rear paw in frustration and bawls a little yelp. Mom comes over and gives comfort; she lies back on the snow and lets the cub nurse. The eerie, distinctive burble of bear suckling floats throughout the basin. The subadult grizzly leaves the water and grazes at the foot of the mountain slope. The cub, leaving his mother a few yards behind, approaches the teenage bear. The tiny cub walks as close as ten feet from the bigger bear. Never before have I seen such behavior here. The mother makes a small move and the subadult bear lopes off into the dead trees and continues feeding a mere 150 feet away. They know each other.

Something odd is happening down there: some sort of social conduct generally unknown in the professional literature of bear behavior.

Out of the timber emerge a grizzly mother and her two brown cubs of the year. The sow is thin and her cubs are tiny. They rush into a far corner of the little lake across from the other grizzly family, who watch attentively. As the skinny mother and her two cubs play, the sow with the single cub enters the pond. Now five grizzlies play in the water, a little tarn across which you might throw a softball. The families watch each other. The mother with two cubs gets out, shakes off the water, and walks nervously counterclockwise around the tarn. They get within forty feet of the other bear family. One of the two cubs approaches even closer, then turns and runs back to mom. Meanwhile, the subadult murmurs a vocalization, perhaps a warning growl, from the near hillside. The grizzly with the single cub retreats to the snow patch and watches.

I can scarcely believe my eyes; a half-dozen grizzlies dance in a seventy-foot circle in the fading light. Then, out of nowhere, a third grizzly family, a dark mother with a large black cub of the year, emerges from the shadow. All eight grizzlies are now in the bottom of the little basin regarding one another. The thin mother bear with her two cubs huddle together, as if they are the least sure of themselves among this singular gathering. The first grizzly family comfortably indulges in play, chewing on each other's ears; the second family with a single cub also plays on the snowbank. This fat cub now runs toward the subadult who stands on the hillside a short distance away. The much larger bear spins and runs away uphill.

It is nearly dark and I am unable to digest this unique spectacle of bear behavior. There is simply no category in which to stack it. Meanwhile, I must climb to the Grizzly Hilton and put up a tent before it gets pitch dark. Otherwise, I might run into a bear in the gloom, maybe even the Black Grizzly—a potentially tragic though appropriate end to one of the best days of my life.

I haul my heavy pack up the last, steep quarter mile of ridge. Finally, the summit. The Grizzly Hilton looms in the dusk.

The Grizzly Hilton is a tiny thicket of spruce and fir atop the summit ridge but apart from the main game (bear) trail tracing the ridgetop. A tiny opening among the stunted trees is big enough for a small tent. I have never found evidence of grizzlies using the thicket as a bear bed. At the same time, to call the location a bear-safe camp would be to stretch the truth. Nor is it the kind of place you can expect to get a decent night's sleep.

I erect my mountain tent and fastidiously position my sleeping bag inside between two root bumps. Just at dark, distant lightning flashes from an isolated thunderhead. As a precaution, I gather twigs and dry grass in a garbage bag. I try never to use fire up here; the kindling is just in case a big bad bear comes nosing around in the middle of the night. Only once has this happened: the Black Grizzly terrorized my tiny fire at the Hilton for six hours.

The wind whips the tent fly, and a few drops of heavy rain slap against it. Three beats of rolling thunder and it's all over. It must be past midnight. The din of wind bothers me; you can't hear the rustle of approaching animals. Wide-awake, I strain to hear the night sounds of the mountain; the distant bugling of a bull elk arrives between deafening blasts of wind. The breeze subsides and the storm passes. In the silence between gusts, I somehow fall asleep.

Morning. The little knob I call the Grizzly Hilton falls off steeply in three directions down thick, brushy slopes. From each bearing comes the high-pitched bugle of elk; about a half-dozen bull elk vie actively for cows. The rut will dominate their lives for the next week or so.

The day is still cool with heavy dew clinging to the yellow grasses, the autumn colors muted with a hint of fog. I pull on my duct-tape-patched down jacket, walk to the edge of the summit, and stare down into the basins below. The big sow with the sleek cub browses on mountain ash berries at the head of the cirque. The two subadults feed on berries only a hundred yards away. In the north basin, a moose stands at the edge of the timber. I see no other bears.

I contour north about fifty feet, noting that the bumper crop of huckleberries at this elevation is already ripe, the bushes drooping under the heavy load. This side hill is the Black Grizzly's favorite foraging area. On the average year, he shows up here late, about the second week of September. I don't know where he comes from or where he spends the rest of his bear year. But when he does arrive at the Hilton, all hell breaks loose, especially when food is scarce. His cantankerous aggressiveness drives most other grizzlies away. This year, with the abundant berries, he seems a little more tolerant. I might add that he tends to treat humans, meaning myself, like other dominant bears. If there's plenty of chow and space, we can peacefully coexist. If not, he tends to eat things that smell like me, sending a most personal message for me to get the hell off his mountain. I always heed it.

Only once years ago did we come nose to nose: we confronted each other at thirty feet on this same ridgeline. It was nearly dark and he had hop-charged half the distance to me in an angry single leap. All this was five minutes after an inconclusive fight during which he tried to kill a sow grizzly and her yearling. Thinking I certainly was going to get it this time, I spoke carefully to the Black Grizzly with the tone of empathy and conciliation. He then flicked his upright ears and gracefully turned away from me, disappearing into the thick undergrowth. The huge bear allowed me to dart by him and race up the ridge to my camp at the Grizzly Hilton—a muscular gift of restraint that remains one of the cardinal experiences of my short life.

That ancient peril, fear of bears, now knocks gently on my door. I sit on a burnt log left over from the 1967 forest fire and listen. Most of the time, I hear the bears before I see them. For five minutes I squat silently. Now and then I think I hear something. The wind is dead and amphitheater-like topography intensifies sound from below. A branch breaks off to the north, and it's not my imagination.

There is a feeding grizzly browsing in the dense brush a hundred yards straight down the steep slope and off to my left, one of the Black Grizzly's choice spots. I put my binoculars on the location and wait. There is a rustle of underbrush. Ten minutes later, a very large, dark brown bear ass pokes out of the elk-high vegetation. The grizzly turns and looks my direction. It's him.

With the Black Griz dominant on the scene, I think it's time for me to split. This afternoon, when most of the grizzlies have bedded, I'll break camp and pack down the ridge, vacating the mountain, leaving it to the bears. I don't want to go but it's the right thing to do. With me up here bumping into bear families and subordinate grizzlies, the odds are increased that one of them could be spooked and run off into that black son of a bitch. Smaller bears could be killed, and it would be my fault.

I sit among the stalks of bear grass, looking out at the distant Continental Divide. God, I hate to leave. The morning sun squints from between distant peaks as I look out on two thousand square miles of forests, glaciers, and river bottoms, a great uninhabited piece of Late Pleistocene landscape. Like Ed Abbey, I consider this is our true home. We call it wilderness, but it's actually just the remnant of the homeland we never entirely abandoned. All our evolution happened in habitats urban people now consider to be wild. Our genome, I think, owes little to the past ten thousand years. We *need* that wildness: that which evolves doesn't last without the enduring conditions of its genesis.

It's near midday; the autumn sun bakes steam out of the old log I'm sitting on. Below in the south basin, all the bears except the medium grizzly and her cub have vanished. I have two concerns: I don't want to retreat down the spur main ridge until all the various families, subadults, and subordinate grizzlies have safely retired to day beds. The safety is as much for them as for myself; should I surprise these bears, there is the chance of running them off into the Black Grizzly. My second concern is the Black Grizzly himself. Where is he? I need to know before hiking out.

I stand and walk along the edge of the ridge, glassing as much of the two basins as I can. No sign of the Black Grizzly, who, though I haven't heard him moving for two hours, could still be right below me in the brush. I drop down the ridge, checking the wind, not wanting my scent to disturb the bears.

A large red-crested bird with a heavy bill alights in a dead snag thirty feet down the ridge. The pileated woodpecker is a familiar sight here as it feeds on the bark beetles that commonly invade lodgepole pine. Sitting quietly listening for the Black Grizzly, I enjoy the companionship of the colorful bird. After twenty minutes or so the woodpecker flies off, and I climb back up to the Hilton.

By now, I'm almost certain the Black Grizzly has bedded. I just don't know where. Before packing up for the trip out, I must make sure that he's not on my exit route. His two favorite bedding spots are below in the timber and way up high, just north of the Grizzly Hilton.

The ridge the Hilton occupies rolls north into a little saddle, then climbs another quarter mile to a major summit. A few thickets of spruce and fir grow along this narrow ridge. From that saddle, I might be able to locate where the big bear is sleeping.

I pack my gear away and stash it in my pack, leaving it behind, ready for the trip out. Moving slowly, I edge north toward the little saddle. The Black Grizzly could be bedded just ahead. The last place I spotted him was directly below the saddle that is now only a hundred feet away. I creep through the brush, leaning my good ear into the breeze, listening for the slightest of sounds, the breathing of a six-hundred-pound grizzly—a terrifying thought, if I had time to think, which I don't.

Grizzlies bed in fairly predictable places: next to trees close to meadow openings, in thickets like alder bottoms, and in clumps of stunted trees at timberline. Three such possibilities exist along this quarter mile of ridge. I ease toward the first of these, a little thicket of conifers a few yards away. Grizzly bears are very secure on day beds. You can get far closer than you want to. Dominant grizzlies sometimes growl a warning while bedded telling you that if you come any closer, and they have to get up and cut their nap short, you'll pay the price.

I shake loose my instincts, my subconscious antennae sweep ahead scanning the mountain for subliminal messages. I reach the saddle where the brush opens up a bit. A steep rocky gully lies across my path. On the other side and uphill a hundred feet, is a second thicket. I'm now receiving signals. I inch across the ravine. A flicker screams an alarm from the basin below. The cry's not for me but intuition tells me I'm in trouble anyway. He's in there. I can sense the bedded grizzly under the trees, and I'm already too close, maybe forty feet. I need to get out of here. I step backward.

I have blundered onto the day bed of the most dangerous animal I personally know on earth. For a second, I savor the crisp mountain air and indulge the fleeting notion that I have never felt more alive. Suddenly, I am aware of an almost imperceptible vibration, a frequency so low I only think I hear it, a resonance in my bones. My skull quivers at the temples. Slowly the sound becomes audible: from the thicket of trees fifteen yards away comes the lowest, deepest growl I have ever heard. Only once before have I been so close to a grizzly on a day bed. That bear, another big male, also growled.

Deep resignation calms but does not paralyze me. Slowly and quietly I back off. The barely discernible growl lingers on the ridgetop, as if blown by a single inexhaustible breath. I turn and ease myself into the gully. It takes me three or four prolonged minutes to soundlessly reach the bottom. I no longer hear the low growl but it really doesn't matter; he's in there waiting to see what I do. I use the gully to stay out of sight and drop east below the ridgeline onto a bear trail tunneling through the underbrush. I contour back a few hundred feet then reemerge on the ridge where I can clearly see the thicket. I put my field glasses on the dark shadows. Faint movement twitches in the dim light. A breeze rustles brown fur. I see the blink of what could be an eyeball.

I quickly retreat to the Grizzly Hilton, tight with emotion, and mechanically ready myself for the trip out. My hand is shaky; I make myself sit down on the heather and breathe deeply. A precarious joy grips my gut like a vise. I am trying to hold on to my wild gift.

The mountains are quiet in the pure afternoon light. Cloudless blue hugs the shadowed ridges. The sun's angle means winter is already on the way. I bounce down the game trail then stop at my observation point above the basins and look back at the saddle where the Black Grizzly slumbers. I flick a military salute: sleep well, old friend. I will dream you in the little death of winter.

12 THE BOMBING RANGE

About halfway west out of Gila Bend on the road to Yuma, my drop-off ride slows and turns onto the off-ramp of highway I-8. The pavement runs back under the interstate to the south then dead-ends on a dirt farm road and a dusty network of abandoned tracks into fallow jojoba fields, the native bean plant used in shampoos and cosmetics, once the yuppie equivalent of a kiwi farm in California.

Now the desert is reclaiming its uncharitable territory. This narrow strip of cultivated land running along the southernmost freeway in Arizona and the adjacent Gila River clings most precariously to a domestic life dependent on irrigation water brought in from the outside; this is the driest, emptiest, most unforgiving landscape in the entire country. The desert here receives only about three inches of rainfall a year. Beyond the abandoned fields, no one lives and no one visits, at least legally. The Sonoran Desert south of here is used by the military as a bombing range—named after a local politician who wanted to bomb the commies back to the Stone Age. This occupies an irregular strip running 125 miles east to west and reaching some thirty or more miles south toward Mexico. The section between here and the Mexican border is the "hot" part of the massive range, the place that gets most of the actual live air to ground rocket and cannon fire.

South of the bombing range lie more empty lands: the Cabeza Prieta Wildlife Refuge, Organ Pipe Cactus National Monument, and the Pinacates, a national park on the Mexican side. Collectively, the area offers the longest linear distance across unoccupied, roadless country in the lower forty-eight. I intend to walk across it.

A deserted, rutted jojoba road at the edge of the great desert dead-ends three miles south of the freeway. I will begin here, walking for a week or more, eventually coming out near Ajo or Organ Pipe Cactus National Monument. I have taken seven of these hikes since 1979, always alone, usually traversing the land end to end, covering maybe 130 or 150 miles, sometimes a little less depending on the route. This trip is different. I plan on traveling due south, on a new route across the hottest part of the range where they do their live firing. This is my first long solo desert walk in many years and the first of any length since I almost bled to death in Nepal. It is also the one walk Ed Abbey and I planned but never took.

I shoulder the big backpack, heavy with three gallon-size canteens of water tied to the frame. It is late afternoon, actually almost sunset. The gullies and eastern slopes of the Aztec Hills are in shadow. I struggle up a low hill, step over the blunted ridgetop, and slide behind the silhouette of the mountain, finalizing the departure from the visible industrial world. Though I can still hear the distant sounds of trucks to the north on the freeway, before me lies an endless expanse of desert hills, bajadas, not another human on the ground until Highway Numero Dos, just south of the international border, a full week's travel.

Off to the east I see a sign marking the boundary of the bombing range. I walk over for a look:

> AVISO! WARNING!
>
> USAF Gunnery Range. Unlawful to enter without permit of the installation commander. (Sec. 21, Internal Security Act 1950, 50 USC 797.) Equipment, ammunition, scrap and bomb fragments are U.S. Government property. Do not remove. Unauthorized personnel found in this area are subject to arrest and search.

Ignoring the warning, I enter without permit and walk south. The sun drops behind an unnamed mountain of the Mohawk Range. A thin lunar crescent, about a day and a half past the new moon, hovers just above the gray horizon. A covey of Gambel's quail squawks in a brushy wash choked with wolfberry. I hear the soft *wurp* of phainopeplas settling into the palo verde trees for the night. About a mile ahead I see another big palo verde surrounded by smaller ironwood trees, marking the course of a sand wash: a good place, with firewood, to camp.

I trudge across the gentle slope of the outlier hills, through creosote and bursage, occasional saguaro cactus and cholla. The light is dim by the time I reach the wash. I dump off the pack and sit down in the sand. Mars is high in the southwestern sky.

The area in and around this bombing range is my favorite place to walk, although I haven't attempted a big walk here since Ed's death. It was also his choice for a long solo stroll. He did two of them here. On Ed's last attempted trek—down in the Growler Valley—he'd had to turn back. "Too weak, too sick," he said, "I just couldn't do it."

In the coolness of the desert wash, I think about him, how he felt, what he thought about that last trip. I am still a bit out of shape since my blood loss in the Himalayas and by being over fifty years old. But when Ed called that last walk quits he was sixty and acutely low on blood. I am a lucky man and know it. Maybe I'll complete the walk and close the loop for both of us. Already I tingle with anticipation: *nights and days alone* in this great arid wilderness.

The Pleiades are overhead. Silence settles over the valley. A great horned owl hoots four times. Minutes later, a smaller owl, probably a screech owl, trills from up the rubble slope of the Aztec Hills. No poor-wills yet; they hibernate and late January is too early for them. I can hear the rumble of the railroad six miles north. No matter, I am moving south, into the immense emptiness, the great desert solitaire.

I kindle a blaze of creosote twigs and add ironwood. When the fire spreads, I sweep coals into a hole surrounded by three rocks I have collected. I balance an aluminum pot filled with a pint of water on the rocks. Dinner is simmered black bean soup with a handful of tsampa dumped in for ballast. I toss a mesquite log on the fire and lie back on my pad, head against my sleeping bag. The sky is alive with stars seen nowhere else on the continent: the moon has set and the clean, arid blackness of the desert sky reveals stellar secrets. These long winter nights encompass more hours than I want to spend sleeping or stargazing (a tent isn't necessary here). I know this from my seven big walks here. I pack a book. Usually a big paperback. One trip, I packed *Moby Dick*, on another, *The Odyssey.* I've also hauled books by Tolstoy, Matthiessen, and Jim Harrison. This trip, for the first time, I'm lugging a hardbound book.

I pull it from my pack, along with a pair of half-moon reading glasses, and screw on the light of a mini-mag flashlight, and try to read a bit. The book is *Hayduke Lives!,* the last book Ed Abbey ever wrote. I think I had held off reading it as I didn't feel like entering such a personal book on the eve of his death and then after. It was too close to home. Now some years have passed.

The first chapter is called "Burial." I read a few pages. It's about the burial of an aged desert tortoise by a huge earth-moving machine named "Goliath."

Although the chapter is but five pages long, I can't finish it: it's just too sad for the likes of this perfect desert night. I have also brought along Abbey's last journal pages, notes recorded on his last desert hikes here on the Cabeza Prieta.

At sunrise a cool breeze blows up from Mexico. I load up quickly and head south. The big Dana backpack claws into my shoulders, and I adjust and cinch up the hip belt. Including the two remaining gallons of water, there's probably about sixty pounds in there. I remember a time when I could carry a hundred. The memory comforts me, and I move along briskly toward the dark basaltic nose of the Aguila Mountains five miles to the southeast. There should be water there. A good rain fell here ten days ago. Damp mud still coats the deeper pockets of the washes.

The desert valley bottoms and slopes—the bajadas—are covered with creosote bushes. Not much else grows out here except when it rains a lot. Among the creosote, low mounds mark the limits of rodent colonies. The ground squirrel population seems to be thriving, especially roundtail ground squirrels. Fresh badger sign is all over the colonial lairs, the spiral grooves of claw marks show where squirrel dens have been excavated. One might not expect to see so many badgers in the low, dry deserts but the years of walking out here have taught me otherwise. This tough little animal is a prodigious digger. Of claw-rakers in the mountain states, only the grizzly bear moves more dirt.

Fresh green filaree thrives in the shade of the larger creosote bushes, explaining the rodent population boom and their badger predators. Bighorn sheep tracks cross the bajadas; I intersect their sign every mile or less. There are also sign of three antelope but no deer or javelina on the flats. Coyotes and bobcats are common here, as are gray and kit fox. Mountain lion are more closely paired with deer or sheep in the mountains and do not frequent these valley bottoms.

I aim for the west buttress of the Aguilas, the "Eagle Mountains." They are a dark block of volcanic rock—basalt or andesite—tilted gently to the northeast. At this easy pace, I'll get there before midday. The morning is cool. A single red-tailed hawk soars by. I walk on, ignoring the minor aches and pains in my back and shoulders, hefting pleasantly all the old memories of hundreds of days spent walking in the Cabeza Prieta desert.

There is not a human sign on the land until I reach the foot of the Aguilas where three targets used by the Air Force are stuck into the bajada like giant paper airplanes. This is the beginning of the "South Tactical Range" of the Barry M. Goldwater Air Force Range, the area of "live fire" that runs from here down into the Growler Valley of the Cabeza Prieta Wildlife Refuge. Earlier this morning I heard rocket and cannon fire coming from the opposite side of the Aguilas. High overhead, two single engine jets scream by, F-16s maybe. This is no surprise. You expect such activity here, though every single time the flyboys buzz or bomb I involuntarily sink to my knees among the creosote, a habit left over from Vietnam. I slide in close to the Aguilas finding an ancient foottrail and watch a pair of twin engine jets, F15Es called "Strike Eagles," blast through the pass that bifurcates the Eagle Mountains.

I tramp on southward, following the prehistoric Indian trail. A pile of potsherds, most of a big oja, lies on the cryptogrammic soil. This pot is the harder-tempered Yuman-made pottery, though both Piman and Yuman-speaking people trekked through this country.

At the big pass in the mountains, I turn east into the interior of the range, because this is where you can find rainwater caught in tanks or tinajas. There are four water places here in the Aguilas, a relatively well-watered desert place. I know this from the old topographic maps, but it would be risky, even potentially fatal, if one should show up alone on foot at one of these tanks only to find it dry. Neither Abbey nor I have ever been this far north in the Aguilas before. Only one person I know has. His name is Bill, and he was a friend of Ed's and is still a friend of mine. Bill confirmed that I could get water at Don Diego and that there was an additional catch basin constructed by the Arizona State Game and Fish Department between twin hills to the southeast, good information because it isn't on any map. Eagle Tank is a natural tank that retains rainwater for months, but it's hard to get to. Thompson Tank is a man-made catchment built by the wildlife refuge. Don Diego is an ancient watering place that has been slightly "improved" by bighorn sheep hunters. Don Diego is where I plan to get my drinking water.

Near the entrance to the gap in the mountains, my eye catches a low north-facing cave, its roof blackened by fire smoke. I investigate. A few petroglyphs beautify the rocks near the entrance, circles and spirals pecked into the patina of andesite. A few potsherds and argillite flakes lie on the floor. A rusted can attests to more recent visitors, probably prospectors from the early part of the twentieth century.

I hike eastward. An antler from a good-sized mule deer lies on an alluvial bench. Hummingbird bush and brittlebush grow in the washes. Black-tailed gnatcatchers flit among the mistletoe. One encilia plant already boasts yellow blossoms. Though it's still January, spring is on the way. Hoofed animals travel through here: deer, a few javelina, and sheep. Most of the tracks are bighorn, in all sizes. The most recent shows a ewe herd of four adults with five smaller sheep traversing this wash since the last rain. There is no recent human sign of any kind.

Up on a cobble terrace are crude circles of stone, rounded boulders the size of melons arranged in ancient rings five to ten feet in diameter. These prehistoric alignments are sometimes called "sleeping circles" though it seems clear they weren't all used for sleeping.

I move on toward the Don Diego Tank, passing more stone circles. Near the mouth of the canyon in which the tank lies, I drop my pack. I remove matches, a snakebite kit, though it's still too cool for rattlesnakes, my canteens, and a .22 Magnum pistol. It feels good to be free of the heavy backpack. I follow a game trail up the canyon. I pass another deer antler and a big rock etched with bighorn sheep petroglyphs. This arid but rich desert habitat, probably unchanged for many centuries, has always supported big game animals. The canyon hooks west into a narrow slot. The water should be there in the shade.

Don Diego Tank is beautiful. It's actually several natural rock basins scoured out by torrential summer monsoons. Even the smaller tinajas have water. I drink a bellyful, fill two gallon-size canteens, and start back down the canyon already in late afternoon shadow.

By the time I return to my pack, the sun is setting. Bighorn sheep sign is everywhere. I make camp in the wash below one of the stone circles among hummingbird bush and between a big ironwood and a palo verde tree. I spread out my sleeping pad and kindle a small fire. My right kneecap hurts. I take 600 mg of ibuprofen; I have been using the anti-inflammatory drug prophylactically as recommended by my aging and aching climber-buddy Yvon Chouinard. Yvon told me to take 600 mg in the morning and wait thirty minutes to let it work. At our age, these little pains are inevitable. I comfort myself thinking our species was evolved to hunt, breed, and then die of old age at thirty-two, and these later decades should be lived, if at all, as a gift.

I do my evening stretching exercises for my lower back. It doesn't hurt half as much as it usually does on these long walks, partly because I have been wearing Clarke Abbey's lightweight binoculars around my neck instead of my usual four-pound Navel WWII field glasses.

I open *Hayduke Lives!* and read four or five short chapters, then lay the book aside and pull out the loose sheets of Abbey's Cabeza Prieta notebooks. I pick out a passage about me written when Ed was camping in the Granite Mountains, which lie only ten miles to my south:

> 1-4-1988, Cabeza Prieta
> And the Peacock problem. Doug is like a brother to me. And maybe that's why, most of the time, I can't stand him. He's too much like me to love. And yet, on the other hand, there's a great zest for life about him, a gusto in living that I lack and bitterly envy. Many love him. He attracts people with magnetic charm.

I find another Cabeza Prieta entry:

> I have now walked 75 miles since Welton [Welton is 35 miles west on the freeway from where I started this walk]. But have seen "nada" of Pinta Mountains (must get to Heart Tank someday).
>
> Five days now I've been living in the open—no roof, no walls. God but I'm stiff and sore, and me poor dogs hurt. How long will it take to get lean and hard and fast again? Too old? What's the difference? That which we are, we are, and if we

> now are less than once we were, still even so we are what few men ever dream or hope to be.
>
> Did Doug deposit Ed 'Rage' Gage out here too?

Abbey meant our friend Edwin Gage for whom I maintain a secret and no doubt illegal memorial only a few miles from where Ed Abbey was (and 35 raven miles southwest of my campfire here) when he wrote those notes. Suddenly, I miss them both, these two friends with whom I did nearly all of my non-solo travel in the Cabeza Prieta.

I read on in the journal:

> 2-27, Cabeza Prieta Wildlife Refuge
>
> "The old bod is breaking down, falling apart, like an old car; one part goes, something else begins to malfunction—gallstones, portal vein obstruction, pancreatitis, burned-out stomach, esophageal varices, high blood pressure, abdominal fluid, anemia, enlarged spleen—and now another kidney stone. thromboses....
>
> Hubris. My debauchery and arrogance have finally overtaken me. Thought I had the world by the balls; now Fate has a hard grasp on "my" balls.
>
> Character and fate: A man's fate is his character (Heraclitus). By the age of forty, a man is responsible for his face (Abbey), and his fate.
>
> I think.
>
> My weight is down to 170. Hyperactive. High-energy illness. The brain keeps going at 90 mph. Hard to get to sleep. Too short for bullshit. Too short for understanding. Too short for my love of wife and children.

The quarter crescent moon has set. The sky is alive with stars. I poke a creosote branch further into the fire. Old Ed struggled, or rather lived with his death for far longer than I knew. Struggle would be the wrong word. All of us will succeed at death very well despite our lack of preparation. My own mortality is no longer tapping at the door, though I know it's out there, just beyond the light of my campfire, waiting. But death is nothing, it's the living, the love, the unfinished work of the world, the joy that holds us here.

Abbey's journal continues:

> 4-4
> Most men fear death, and resist it, and invent pathetic, vain consolations to outwit death. But it is possible to accept the idea of one's own death, without embracing it, by seeing the death of the individual as a intrinsic, essential, natural part of the great life process.

I push a last ironwood stick on the fire and fade off while watching the flickering light.

In the morning I eat a Power Bar and load up my gear. I head due west through another gap in the mountains leading to the San Cristobal Valley. I pass more circles of stone. A flaked quartzite chopper lies in the center of one of them. Rust and pale-green lichen on the stones attests to relative antiquity. I pass another set of deer antlers and turn south along the western front of the Aguilas. A-10 Warthogs scream by overhead. The tank killers maneuver against the contours of the desert topography. They are very flexible flying machines that wasted thousands of Iraqi vehicles and their crews in the Gulf Wars. I hear live fire over the ridge to the southeast, hitting the ground near a target area maybe five miles away.

Fifty-caliber casings, slugs, and linkage litter the desert floor here and there but, in truth, there's not a lot of ordinance lying around. When I consider the impact of the military bombing range measured against the kinds of activities it has precluded—mining, off-the-road vehicles, and livestock grazing—I think more kindly on the flyboys up there. I pick up a dud fifty-caliber round and remember a time back in Vietnam in the spring of 1967 when I was learning to use this weapon —the defensive fifties at our A-camp in Thuong Duc—and how I practiced on the bombed-out steeple of a Catholic church (used by VC snipers) two klicks distant. I finally got good enough to drop a tracer or incendiary round in the window of the steeple a mile away, but the Vietnamese priest came up from the resettlement village and asked us to stop practicing on the ruins of his church.

I walk on. Five minutes later I see an unexploded 500-pound bomb lying out on the bajada. Nearby is a detonating device. It reads:

Warning Explosive device
RR 141 E/AL; 1370-01-234-0718; 8122814-1;
Do not rotate this lever —>

This time I heed the warning.

The man-made water catchment at Thompson Tank is covered by a galvanized roof, which shields the precious liquid from evaporative sunlight. I pry up the edge far enough to dip my canteen cup inside and fill my canteens. I pass another set of deer antlers and a disarticulated skeleton of a bighorn ewe. A low gap in the mountains leads east and I take it.

I veer south through another pass, following an ancient trail. Painted black-on-buff pottery litters the centuries-old pathway.

I camp a mile south of the Aguilas, near a little outlier hill, and turn in early. About 9 PM, the eastern sky is alit with parachute flares, which illuminate the desert with their slow-drifting eerie light. The light show goes on for an hour.

The next day it is almost noon when a helicopter shows up for some target practice, using rockets and mini-guns. There have been A-10s firing all morning so it is nothing out of the ordinary. Abruptly, I hear a stray round ricocheting along the desert floor. I automatically hit the ground, waiting for the next round to come crashing through the creosote, forgetting where I am, awaiting the heavy soft slug, in slow motion now, the huge weight on my chest, the heaviness turning to excruciating pain as I have imagined it thousands of times.

Then I am alone in the great desert. Spared once again, the survivor. Little me. Luck?

There is always the temptation to see your own survival as a clear reflection of the favor of the gods. Fortunate and favored, the survivor stands in the midst of countless fallen comrades. For the buck sergeant, outlasting your buddies may produce guilt; but for the modern masters of war, I think, for the generals, it is the unblocking of power. The greater the number of dead, the bigger the heap of bodies, the more clearly the favor of the gods confirms their invulnerability. After Hitler survived the bomb designed to take his life, that killed almost everyone in the room except him, he concluded: "Providence had kept me alive to complete my great work." The butcherous trails left by the compulsive campaigns of kings, dictators, and generals confirm this murderous pride.

For me, this observation born of experience and triggered by memory is neither distant nor esoteric. Here on the Barry M. Goldwater Air Force Range, the evil bears names. The only four star general I ever had the misfortune to be forced to shake hands with was General William C. Westmoreland, a bad general, a tactical dunce, a murderous idiot whose Norman Rockwell banality in his starched fatigues at Thuong Duc belied the bloodiest hands in Vietnam. This man, who wanted to use tactical nuclear weapons to defend his blunder at Khe Sanh and to this day thinks the Tet Offensive was a great American victory, caused the deaths of thousands of human beings—American and Vietnamese soldiers, civilian women and children—and I will not forgive him. I hold him directly responsible for the killing of my friends and comrades at Lang Vei. He is accountable *right now* and to me for the death of Moreland, Dinh Pho, and my other Hre brothers on February 7, 1968.

I look at my hands. Alone, forty miles from the nearest human, I am shaking with rage and grief. When we know what a single death can mean to a family, even what the death of my friend Ed Abbey, who was prepared for the journey, means to me, how can anyone countenance these butchers?

I open my eyes to the great desert valley. We carry our crimes like the tortoise carries its shell. No clean slates for murderers. Robert MacNamara's confessions come too late. My pragmatic forgiveness of earthly sin does not extend to those who slaughter children; they do not get to start a new life, free of culpability, on my planet.

Today, under fire from the high-tech weapons practiced on the bombing range, a warrior's skill no longer counts. It's a mind-boggling potluck to avoid the potlatch of the dead. Ed Abbey is gone and I'm still here. Why and to what end?

Silence returns to the bajada. I take several deep breaths and move on. I am over-reacting to the risk of live fire, a stray round, or an unexploded bomb; it's nearly nil, about the same as a lightning strike. But why take the risk at all?

Because it's worth it.

Now I head due south, anxious to leave the live bombing behind, toward the tip of the Granite Mountains, to the same spot Abbey and I passed through just before New Year's Day in 1974. A lot of years out here. A lot of walks. This could be my last. You never know. But I'm getting close to what I came out here for, close to my own mortality, close to old Ed, close to the fire and the source of life. On my previous walks across the Cabeza Prieta, there was always something lurking in the back of my mind, some personal baggage. This time is different. I love my children and miss them, but I am where I want to be. I may be old, I think, but Christ I'm still capable of enjoying every step of this walk. It sure as hell is not for everyone, but for me, it's like childhood: precisely, a childish indulgence, here in the place where it all started, each yard of ground fresh with the sweet smell of discovery pouring off the desert.

I pass an ocherous outlier, Red Point Hill. Most of the little hills here don't have names. In a wash running close to the rocks, I can smell the wet red clay now drying into pentagonal mud cracks.

Ahead, a point of rock and a broad belt of mesquite mark the run of a major drainage, Growler Wash. Another 500-pound bomb lies not too far from two unexploded 250s. The pack bites into my shoulders but I don't mind. I am carrying enough water to see me to Charlie Bell Well in case I find no standing water in Growler Wash.

Growler Wash heads up in the San Cristobal Valley, drains southeast around the north end of the Granite Mountains, then runs due south toward Mexico between the Granite and Growler Mountains. Down there somewhere, Ed Abbey is buried.

I pick my way through a thicket of mesquite and thorn trees and step out into the desert arroyo. Potsherds and fire-broken rock litter the edges of the broad wash. Farther out in the middle, I see what looks like a sea turtle shell. I walk over and flip the big turtle-shaped rock on its back. The rock is a huge metate, a sixty-pound grinding bowl used by the ancient Hohokam to grind wild seeds, mostly mesquite and palo verde here. I explore the area. It is a large archeological site. The Hohokam Indians trekked down this way a thousand years ago on their walk to Bahia Adair on the Sea of Cortez to gather clam shells, which facilitated dreams. Red-on-buff pottery and fragments of glycymeris shell are everywhere. A big bird, what we used to call a "marsh hawk," twists over the bajada. I find four more fifty-pound metates. This area was also used for bombing practice more than fifty years ago. At the south end of the Hohokam site, four hulks of 1940-vintage cars used as targets are twisted into rusted wreckage, blasted to pieces. Thousands of .30 and .50 caliber and one-inch slugs litter the sand. The remains of innumerable napalm containers are scattered throughout the area.

This place is more beat up from live fire than any other spot I've seen on the entire bombing range.

Now I remember that Ed and I were here a long time ago.

Growler Wash is drier than I expected; lots of mud but no standing water. The creosote has been burned and blasted by WWII napalm; there has been much erosion and some damage to the prehistoric archeological site. Potsherds, fire-cracked rock, and obsidian flakes lie along more recent relics of contorted lead and steel-jacketed slugs. I will name it the Bullet Site. Two single engine jets scream over. The fucking planes wear on you.

I look around. I've been here twice before but it looks different now. My first trip through was with Ed Gage twenty-some years ago. A couple years later, Abbey and I came through with my dog Larry. I shake my head. I still grieve.

At the lower end of this site, Growler Wash bends around a hill of basalt. Some volcanic faces wear a fine patina the color of oxidized blood. It would be a perfect place to find ancient petroglyphs. But there are none. The occurrence of rock art everywhere in America, and especially in the Southwest, is never quite random. From all considerations Western, this looks like a good place. But apparently not. Something unfortunate or terrible might have happened here, even before the military bombed the shit out of it.

Late afternoon now and I continue down the valley. Five small outlier hills are perched just on the east side of the bajada, roughly in a line, perhaps reflecting the way lava rose from an ancient fault. The hills beckon; they are the only breaks in the smooth terrain of the valley. I would like to visit them, though they are one of three target areas that the Air Force has bombed and strafed with live fire during the past two days. Maybe I can sneak over there in the morning before the jets are up and about.

I camp eight seconds times the speed of sound from the hill I want to visit. I know because just before dark, Warthogs shriek across the valley, shatter the deep silence, and blast the hell out of my hill with white phosphorous rockets. One A-10 banks slowly, seemingly hovering in place over the bajada, then methodically flies directly toward me at the level of the tops of the ironwood trees. The dark menacing aircraft appears to approach with the deliberate steps of an aggressive peccary—or warthog. I look up as he passes and can see a face in the cockpit. Had he seen me, my little camp? Would it make any difference if he had?

The military exercise goes on until dark. The rockets give way to parachute flares, reminding me of nights in Vietnam, when our A-camps would come under mortar attack and the C-47 "Spooky" gunships would arrive from Danang and provide us with illumination so we could see the Vietcong sappers on the barb wire.

Within a few minutes of the departure of the planes, it is hard to believe the quiet. Nothing human as far as the eye can see. No sounds until coyotes cut into the solo of a great horned owl. Though I came out here knowing as well as anyone what the bombing range is like, experienced from the ground (on foot without entry permit), the intrusive magnitude of the modern military machinery still staggers me. The flip side is that it's the wildest desert place I can find when the planes are silent. Both subjects, war and wilderness, are close to my heart.

I settle into the wild desert night, kindle a little blaze, make some soup, then slide into my sleeping bag next to the fire. I pull out *Hayduke Lives!* and read for an hour, then turn to the transcription of Ed's Cabeza Prieta notebooks, finding a passage about a party he threw for me:

> 5-27
>
> ...a going-away party for Peacock. I'm getting too obsessed with this literary career biz. I should write my good nuvvie, then quit, take up shoe repair, horses, masonry, something useful, honest and sensible "while time remains."

> 6-6
> Lethargy. Sadness. I think I'm dying.
>
> 7-7
> Longing, longing, longing—for what? Death. I wish I were dead. There, I said it, and it's false. I cannot go now. I have two sweet daughters, a young wife.

Ed wrote all this years before he died, years before I knew he was going to die. A small pygmy owl whistles from a saguaro. There's a lot of death in Ed's journals. I come to an older passage, written just after my son's first birthday on 2-8-85, about Abbey's own funeral, his burial instructions, how he needs a death certificate for the legal stuff, and requests for his own wake:

> . . . Doug and his guns.

He had thought it all out.

I didn't know back in 1985 that Ed was living so closely with death. I am suddenly ashamed of the careless way I treated the people I've loved, the utterly slothful mismanagement of the simple elements of my daily life, the squabbling. The quarreling never came to blows, except sort of, one of those times when Ed again moved in a bit too soon after I had broken up with a girlfriend and it cost him sixty bucks—later quite laughable—in chiropractic adjustment.

I read on:

> I feel no fear of death. (Perhaps because I do not fully believe in death.) But I do feel a great sadness, an irremediable sorrow, at the possibility that I may not live long enough to help our Rebecca become a girl, a teen-ager (another insolent teen-ager!), a woman. That thought hurts. Otherwise . . . I

> might say—enough. Enough. Enough! Sick, sick, I'm sick of being sick. Will I never regain full health? Down to 165 pounds at this time. I'm a wreck, a wrack, a specter of me former self. (I dream of great walks . . .)

I close the book over the notebook pages and settle into my sleeping bag. I stare into the embers of the campfire. I sleep. The dreams come again—jaguars, tigers, bears—all of them in a night's dreaming. There is no fear in my dreams now. Ever since returning from the Sierra Tarahumara, Nepal, and the Grizzly Hilton these animal dreams have taken a more nourishing turn, tied to actual and spiritual birthing—strengthening my attachment to the mother earth, looking to the moon where the dreams come from, the moon in the belly, the feminine.

During the long desert night, my father tries to return to me in dream.

I wake to a flawless desert sky. A canyon wren's crystalline notes drift down from a rocky outlier. The flyboys aren't active yet. I want to walk south far enough down the Growler Valley to get beyond the live fire zone. Though I'm still curious and want to visit the five little outlier hills, the aircraft and military exercises are grating. I'm glad to have walked fifty miles without crossing sign of modern humans, but the relentless buzzing of aircraft is wearing me down. I want to walk beyond war.

The small hills out in the bajada lie on the eastern slope, about a mile from Growler Wash. I figure I'll walk down the east side of the bosque south and get water at either Sheep Tank or Charlie Bell Well. That will bring me within five or six hundred yards of the hills, which are often used as targets. If I don't see any sign of live fire, maybe I'll sneak over there for a look.

I cross Growler Wash and edge out into the valley. Moments later, A-10s swoop over the ridge and blast hell out of the south hill. The Warthogs fly slowly over me, turning upside down, firing cannons. I contemplate hiding. If the pilots don't know I'm here they might drop a bomb on me by accident. If the flyboys see me, they might use me as a target. In the old days, when Abbey and I first started coming out here, they most certainly would have blown you away. In those days, they shot at bighorn sheep, wetbacks, anything that moved and broke the monotony of chasing paper targets. Nobody is supposed to be down here. All activity is illegal. Now, with the New Army, the caring military, their new sensitivity, I guess the odds of being intentionally shot to be about 50-50. This much is true: If they see you and they want you, they can have you. Just beyond where the boys are shooting, a border patrol plane turns northeast over the Growler Mountains. Looking for me? I've heard the BP has placed seismic/acoustic sensors along the border of Mexico and along key routes leading north. Maybe I triggered one. These sensing devices were developed at my old alma mater, the University of Michigan, and were first field-tested in Vietnam during the siege of Khe Sanh and the Tet Offensive. The man for whom this bombing range is named, Senator Barry Goldwater, said back then about the sensors: "One of the greatest steps forward in warfare since gunpowder."

How I loathe these people. I walk on, fifty pounds of gear and water on my backpack, away from the machines of war.

I am about a half mile southwest from the last hill when an F16 drops two bombs a quarter of a mile south of the target, only about three or four hundred yards from me. To let me know he could have me? It doesn't matter. I continue walking. Even if the shrapnel comes close, I won't hit the dirt for these scumbags. I refuse to let these well-armed punks intimidate me. Being willing to die has always imbued people like myself or Abbey with a certain edge. Fuck you jet jockeys. I consider breaking out my .22 pistol for anti-aircraft use. I sure do hate to be defenseless. The only place I never carry guns is grizzly or jaguar country where you don't need one. I walk south. The war is over, I say to myself, the war is over.

It is true. My war is over. I am free to channel that ferocity in new ways, to bring back a piece of this wild gift to those people I love. I will become, have been becoming, a better father. A better husband? Maybe next time.

The border patrol plane doesn't return. Of course, I'm heading south, the wrong direction for an illegal alien or smuggler. By mid-morning the valley is quiet again. I trudge along the mesquite bottom. It's a beautiful morning. A crisp breeze carries up from old Mexico. Nightshade bushes are flush with purple blooms. The phainopeplas are about. A covey of Gambel's quail flushes from the brittle yellow stalks of last year's crop of globe mallow. House finches and flycatchers perch in the mesquite and a Le Conte's thrasher flies from a palo verde tree. I have been watching what looks like a tern or gull soar above the bajada on and off for half an hour. Finally the bird glides close enough for me to focus Clarke's field glasses on its belly and back. The white bird is a kite, probably a Mississippi kite though this is beyond its normal range. Channels of mud linger in the deeper shade of the wash but there is no standing water. Lots of antelope have passed through, and I cross one set of bighorn ram tracks trekking east, toward Sheep Tank.

By late morning, I leave the bombing range behind and cross over the invisible line into the Cabeza Prieta Wildlife Refuge. I find a big ironwood tree in a sandy channel of the main wash. I drop my pack in the shade and lie down in the dirt, using the pack as a pillow. The planes have also retired for siesta. There is no sound beyond the gentle wind, the buzzing of bees, and the midday laughter of quail migrating to a new feeding site within their territory. The incomparable blue of the Arizona sky is laced with high streaked cirrus clouds, just the slightest hint of horsetails.

I wake with the sun on my Montrail boots. The sun has moved about thirty degrees—a two hour nap! I have no schedule to keep. I'm drowsy and don't feel like walking just yet. I take out *Hayduke Lives!* and remove Ed's desert journal notes:

6-20
I've been off my cough syrup (codeine) habit for a week now, but it still hurts. Withdrawal symptoms every evening when I get the run-down miserable flu-like ache-all-over feeling. Beer does not help. Nor coffee nor ice cream. What to do? Heave to and ride her out. Tough it out, like a cowboy or sailor should.

8-3
Trouble, trouble, trouble. Except for sweet things like Clarke and Rebecca, my life seems to me a dismal failure. Good Christ! 58 years old and I've never learned to do "anything practical, useful, sociable." I am becoming a cranky, bitter embittered, dyspeptic old fart...I feel so goddamn inadequate, weak, helpless, inept, slobbish.

GLOOM...and DOOM. Consumed in self-loathing. Bitterness. Disgust with the world of literature, politics, art. Makes a fella want to walk away over the horizon, find a comfortable canyon, lie down, curl up, fade out....

Stop this sniveling! You have work to do, a good wife to support, a beautiful child to help raise! For the love of life, man, drag yourself up out of this slough of despondency!

OK.

9-12
Summer's over here! Hooray! A delightful tingle of autumn in the air. One's thoughts stray to another walk across the Cabeza....

I walk on down the Growler Valley. The deflation of the bajada by rain and wind has mixed fragments of fire-broken rock of many ages. Soon I see pottery, lithic flakes, and pieces of clam shell: another Hohokam site. I pluck a fine crescent of glycymeris rim from the playa. These sea shells, carried inland hundreds of miles on foot across the fiercest desert on the continent, are the raw material of dreams. The ancients carved these crescents, hoops, and cores into holy objects, magic bracelets, and effigies of amphibians.

The Indian site extends south a quarter of a mile. At the far end the exploded detonating device from a bomb lies on the desert pavement. I extract a copper fuse wire and carefully wrap it around two long crescents of ancient clam shell carved out by the Hohokam. I stuff the shells inside a side pocket of my pack, padded by a sock.

By late afternoon I have only covered seven or eight miles. I need to decide if I am to water at Sheep Tank or Charlie Bell Well. I look up at the black wall of the Growler Mountains. Sheep Tank is up there, up seven hundred feet over treacherous scree and ankle-breaking basaltic boulders. A boulder not far from the tank is etched with a name and enigmatic inscription: "John Moore 1909 Was it worth it?" The tank itself is only four miles away, as the raven flies. Charlie Bell is a half dozen miles but on the flat. My feet hurt. I check my water supply: about two and a half quarts. I'll make camp and walk into Charlie Bell Well tomorrow.

The oblique sunlight illuminates a mosaic of green and black on the steep west-facing slope of the Growlers. Where the rock is sufficiently stable to allow for the growth of vegetation, the grass and pale-green lichen appear to be lit from within. The mottled hillside is a lizard skin tapestry of black streaks of recent basaltic slides. I sit and watch the mountains until the shadow creeps up the slope embracing the reptilian landscape.

It is such a great day to be alive. Of all my walks, this one resonates most with the prime elements of my life: wildness and solitude, an experience so original, so fiercely involved with the land, a place so inaccessible that it precludes any notion of recreation—occasionally so wild and hard that it approximates the ordeal of combat without the unforgettable shit-stench of human fear. Here, the fullness and the inexorable circle of life gravitating toward the grave are unaffected.

I climb up the gentle slope of the bajada until volcanic boulders from the mesa above make walking difficult. It is nearly sunset. I find a broad bend in a deep wash and make camp under an ironwood tree. Dinner is tsampa and black bean soup again. Just before dark, I build up the fire and settle in with Ed Abbey's journal:

> 9-25
> According to (Doctor) MacGregor, me blood count is back within normal range. All the same, I feel kinda weak and puny most of the time. My guts are a mess. Tired every evening. "Un" sociable; conversation is a wearisome chore. I'm not sure I'll live to see sixty. So?
>
> Got the world by the tail—with a down-hill pull.
>
> 1-1
> Despondency. Had a quarrel with my dear Susie last night, a quarrel over nothing, really, and today I feel lower than whale shit.
>
> ("Will I never know joy again"?)
>
> Some days it seems like everything goes wrong. I awake with my heart gripped by dread—fear—terror. Of what? I don't know. That's the dreadful fearful terrifying thing about it.
>
> Suicide is an always-viable option. The sensible solution. A rational alternative. Workable compromise.
>
> 5-15
> It's true: In old age, like Byron, my thoughts turn more and more to avarice, less and less to sex, art, adventure and new ideas.
>
> Ol' rockin' chair done got me.
>
> Dis-ease. Thank Gawd for cough syrup. Codeine . . . Furthermore, without death, life would lose half its drama. Joy would seem pallid, beauty pale, danger insipid, adventure empty.

Our existence would become merely spiritual—off white and ghostly. Sort of—idyllic but boring.

Boredom, in fact, would become the "terror." . . . Faced with death, the body recoils in fear, in horror, in terror. The body "knows." The pious pray, but the body "knows."

Face to face with death. To look death in the face—see it, know it—and then . . . go on. The heroic stance.

Exasperation will take ten years off me life.

10-24
My heart is heavy. Very heavy. Opus 132 by lvb. suits my mood exactly. Music—my rampart. Good ol' Ludwig, old courage-giver, hero of Western man.

I remember decades ago when I first played this Beethoven quartet for Ed on the rim of Escalante Canyon in Southern Utah. The journal entry surprises me; I didn't know he was so fond of the Opus 132. It's probably my single favorite piece of music. I need courage. I want to take strength from a hero.

On the other hand, Ed's despondent wail, "Will I never know joy again?" resonates in the desert silence. I remember that void, numb with anguish and pain, after my father died. My dad was exceedingly grieved by the news of my divorce. He loved his grandchildren more than anything. Mom told me how he would go into his room every day and weep. He did this for two months, then he died. The calcified aneurysm he had lived with for over forty years suddenly let go. He died in a stunning spot, the hill country east of Sonoma, California, one of the few pastoral landscapes on earth that grips my eye with its undeniable beauty. I inherited his stash of vitamins; dad had been a disciplined vegetarian and health addict the last years of his life. So I knew he was trying hard to live. I wince.

I have sometimes wondered if I would find joy again. I do when spending time with my children or in wild places like this.

But I also want to fall in love again. The interest, even libido, are intact. So I am open to it. Yet some ambivalence has crept into notions of romance, perhaps a delicate wounding. I have imagined myself frail, a bit tentative in my fifties, unsure of my physical presence, but with an open heart. Ed would have understood. I know, too, that my masculine fragility is a cultural laceration, a mere scratch that will soon itch with the healing of desire.

I might try a new life. I have my work. In the tradition of old Abbey, I write and fight for wild causes. My trip from Tiburón and beyond, to Nepal and the Grizzly Hilton, has opened up all possibilities. I have nothing left over to lose from that journey. I walked it off. I dream the hope of joy.

Two owls hoot from the desert. One is a great horned, the other, some owl that likes to speak in a series of twin hoots. I lie in my sleeping bag smelling mesquite coals on the fire and watching the Dog Star until I fall asleep.

Five hours later, I wake with the flush of a beautiful vision crossing over from my subconscious. I've been graced with another mildly confusing jaguar dream. The dream is less ethereal than sensuous but this is sufficient. I toss a mesquite log on the embers of my fire. In a few minutes, the flames flicker.

In the morning I stuff my gear into the backpack and prepare for the walk to Charlie Bell Well. I am down to less than two quarts of water, actually closer to one, and I like to have a pint or two in reserve in case I break a leg or get nailed, as I once did here, by a rattlesnake.

I wind through an increasingly rocky landscape of volcanic boulders. Crossing a gully, I spot a gray fox watching me. A coyote den is dug into the side of a wash below a thicket of wolfberry. The ocotillo is all leafed out. Indeed, it appears that the Growler Mountains have received twice as much rain as the deserts to the west. The northerly slopes are thick and green with lupine bush.

By afternoon, a number of ancient paths converge toward Charlie Bell. Some are the game trails of sheep, deer, antelope, or range cattle; are routes once traveled by prehistoric Indians. There has probably always been water there.

I follow one of the trails slowly up through the basalt. Climbing up to a little pass from which I should be able to see the windmill at Charlie Bell, I drop my pack and ease forward. Just over the horizon I see white animals against the black of the Growlers. I take out Clarke Abbey's binoculars and squat behind a leafed-out ocotillo plant. The long-legged animals look like some exotic species of domestic goat except they are pronghorn antelope. Ten antelopes, six of which are males, browse fresh green ocotillo leaves. They reach up, so daintily, like gazelles. I watch the antelope for a half an hour, until the sun begins to set. The pronghorn haven't seen me yet. I'm hoping I can drop down a gully to Charlie Bell without disturbing them. I have to get water before dark.

At my first move, the antelope look up at me. Shit. They begin to mill and move east, finally breaking and running among the rugged hillside boulders as gracefully and smoothly as the red-tailed hawk soaring above.

Dropping into the big wash below the well, I unload my pack in the sand. It's getting dark, and I need to get water. The well must be only a half-mile away. I turn my sleeping bag inside out so the white lining shows, then drape it over a tall bush on the bank of the wash so I can find my pack when I come back in the dark.

I climb out of the big, steep-sided wash and pick up the old road to the well. Vehicular travel is prohibited here now, though there is a jeep trail to the rim above, only three miles away. I'm not ready to see people for a couple of days yet so I plan to shoot in, get my water, and hightail it back down the valley before anyone spots me. This time of day, no one will be out here.

Out of ancient habit, I approach the well cautiously. I listen to the birds and crickets: no one around. Charlie Bell Well pumps water into a tank and then into a cement trough. Someone from the federal wildlife service has bolted a lid on the catchment so human visitors can't get to the fresh water. I happen to have a pump, hose, and filter so this is no problem for me but these bureaucratic urban fools just don't get it. Desperate people fleeing murderous Central American death squads come through here. The Feds should acquaint themselves with the history of Tule Well where a Mexican set up shop selling water for fifty cents a drink and the first man through shot him dead. Out here, and for good reason, people will kill for water.

I return and find my pack in the dark. It's later than my accustomed bedtime and I'm tired. Finding a private lid on the precious water so necessary to all life here, human and otherwise, has sullied my good mood. I'm glad no one is around to receive my crabbiness. I read a page of Abbey's notebooks for comfort.

> 1-23
> Doing work I don't want to do so we can live in a way I don't want to live.
>
> 4-19
> I am becoming a cranky old man. Quite. Ex-tremely contentious. True. Quarrelsome, petulant and exceedingly irritable. Right. I have less and less patience with fools, bores, pedants and crooks. I do not love, respect or admire the human race. I think modern history is a horror story, I fear for the lives of my children. I regret and am outraged by the systematic destruction of the natural world for the sake of human greed. Exactly.

Early the next morning I leave my pack behind and revisit the vicinity of Charlie Bell. I want to have a look around and then split early enough in the day to avoid any hikers. From reading the human sign last night, it appears that day hikers visit the well a couple of times a week. Sometimes, illegal immigrants from Mexico hike up the valley and water at Charlie Bell but that's less common.

The wash below the well is alive with birds: flycatchers, pyrrhuloxias, hooded orioles, many hummers, and canyon wrens. It looks like someone has recently tried to pry off the lid of the watering trough. Probable desperate illegal aliens on foot. I consider finishing the job for them and look around for something stiff enough to lever up the plywood lid. I locate an old railroad tie and pick it up. A giant desert hairy scorpion is under it. I gently replace the tie without crushing the scorpion. A shafted flicker sounds an alarm, like they do in grizzly country when something is moving. I look around. Nothing. No sign of the ten antelope today.

Morning sunlight creeps over the rim and floods the basin. I strip off my clothes and walk northeast into the basaltic boulder field where the petroglyphs are. Ed and I came through here in my pickup in 1973, when Ed told me he wanted to be reincarnated as a buzzard. I try to find Abbey's vulture petroglyph. This was where he told me to go visit the Great Galley at Barrier Canyon. I poke around the rock art for a half hour. There are petroglyphs of rain, lightning, and clouds—big thunderheads. I find the big metate that my friend, who ran the Legal Defense Fund for the Sierra Club, and his son found when I brought them out on the eve of the Persian Gulf War, successfully talking the son out of immediately enlisting, six months before the same friend was killed in a car crash.

It has been years since I lost Abbey, a dozen more since Gage killed himself, twenty years since I lost my dog, married, and fathered Laurel and Colin. There were other events but those are the ones that stuck: not much, really, in twenty years, not that much loss, except sometimes, when I think of the life unlived, the stones unturned, the richness that could have been.

I look around the desert valley. It looks just like it did when I came through here with Gage and Abbey. Only the land lasts. Birds and animals and humans come and go, passing through as a thunderhead before the sun.

As the shadows shrink before the rising sun, I prepare to leave. From high on the cliffs above, I hear the clatter of scree falling. Bighorn sheep are moving to day beds. I scan the slopes. I see no sheep but I know they are up there. In the sand below the well, ants drop palo verde leaves in the print of a big cat, a mountain lion of perhaps seventy-five pounds. The day is heating up but still pleasant in the coolness of the wash. On the rising thermal, four turkey buzzards drift. I shoulder my pack and start south, a full load of water and gear, but less than the sixty pounds I started with.

Ironwood, euphorbia, wolfberry, and hummingbird bush grow in the wash bottom. A wave of déjà vu sweeps over me. I am haunted by landscapes, the reoccurring images of places that drift through my dreams and startle my daydreaming. One of those is right here, this sacred desert. Sometimes magical wild animals live in the dream and spill over into the physical landscape like jaguars and cougars. I look around; I know the lion is watching me.

The south end of the Growler Valley is the most beautiful Sonoran Desert country I have ever seen. I make camp early, anxious to explore without the full backpack. The valley is bordered on the west by the Granite Mountains. My camp is not far from the spot where the rattlesnake nailed me in the calf one warm winter night on one of my big solo walks. No one knew I was out there except for Ed who was waiting for me in his truck with Clarke at Papago Well fifteen miles southwest. I managed to hobble in on my own. Neither Ed nor I wanted to be rescued by the Feds out here. We would take our chances; either our friends would come looking or we would perish. Ed and I had that sort of understanding with each other. After all, it was in the wilderness that we were at our best.

That night, I read the last of Ed's notebook entries:

> 1-3-88
>
> Cabeza Prieta: I want to live. Clarke, Susie, Becky and Benjamin need me for at least ten more years. So I must hang on and in there for another decade.
>
> (But how? Black stool again.)
>
> 1-4-88
>
> Every one of my books since "Brave Cowboy" has stayed in print, and every single one has sold by now at least 50,000 copies. Not bad for the most hated, reviled and ignored of modern American writers.
>
> Morning,—Granite Mountains, Cabeza Prieta. Cold water and fresh fruit for breakfast. What a horrible way to begin the day. What I crave is sugar, grease and caffeine. The rotten habits of a soft lazy corrupt life—but mine!
>
> So it's fucking Monday morning again. So what? I think I'll stay out here all fucking winter, slay a few deer, a few sheep, cook their brains and eat their guts. Be happy, healthy and hermit. The wilderness is our only true and native home.
>
> Smog in the valley between here and the Growler Range. Fucking Phoenix. Fucking LA. Fucking techno-industrial culture. You know what? I wish Doug Peacock would suddenly appear, looking for me.

Well, Ed, I say to myself lying next to my fire, I'm a little late, as usual, but I got here. You won't believe it Ed, I say to the smoke, but I cleaned up my act some, worked myself back into decent health. My "gusto for life" has been channeled into being a good father. And that anger—Hayduke's raised fist—Ed, I'm trying to let it go. I walked off a good deal of it, walked away from a lot of war out on the bombing range. But twenty-five years of war-related rage is too much. It takes a toll. The war lasted too long.

The next day, I pack up and prepare to leave the valley. My work, my last big walk, is nearly finished. I take my time, enjoying the walking. I note the change in vegetation: a few *Bursera fagaroides* and torote bushes. I startle a colorful summer tanager in a euphorbia. Two buzzards float on a thermal. I walk up a little canyon then climb out to a tiny flat where I dump off my backpack.

Ed Abbey is buried here. I dig out the packet from the side pocket of my pack and kneel before a torote bush. I repair the wind chime, adding the thin crescents of clam shell for the missing slivers of volcanic glass, using thin copper detonator fuse wire from the 250-pound bomb duds to replace the sunlight-ravaged nylon thread that dangled needles of obsidian from a devil's-claw seed pod—an offering by Ed's sister-in-law, Susan, and her husband, Steve, who dug this grave. Deer or sheep have browsed the small ocotillo tree that was planted by the lead singer of Tucson's best Sonoran white band.

The clan has gathered. A native boulder of basalt wearing a lovely bronze patina stands below the palo verde bush at the top of the little draw. The ground around the boulder is piled high with sea shells, especially glycymeris (do the dead dream?), crystals, and many heart-shaped rocks placed here by children—Ed's children, the singer's children, my children.

I stare at the boulder. The boulder stares back. Chiseled into the rock:

Edward Paul Abbey
1927 – 1989
"No Comment."

THE END

DOUG PEACOCK

A Midwesterner by birth, Doug Peacock volunteered for an intense combat tour in Vietnam as a Green Beret medic. Like many of his fellow soldiers, he returned home, greatly changed, to an equally troubled America. Happenstance joined him up with a group of "desert rats," wilderness anarchists led by Edward Abbey.

Abbey subsequently based George Washington Hayduke, the central character in his bestselling environmental classic, *The Monkey Wrench Gang*, on Peacock. Despite their stormy, almost father-and-son, relationship, Abbey and Peacock traveled and explored the earth's wildest places, including the Cabeza Prieta desert and the Escalante wilderness.

After burying his friend and mentor in the Southwest desert in 1989, Peacock embarked on a risky trail of adventure and discovery. With his war experiences returning with a fury and his domestic life completely unraveling, he turned to the wilderness to challenge death and to save his life.

Peacock is widely known for *Grizzly Years,* an account of many seasons spent studying the grizzlies of the West. He has become an articulate environmental individualist writing about and dedicated to preserving the planet's last remaining wilderness. He lives in Livingston, Montana with his wife, writer Andrea Peacock.

Top: Hayduke by R. Crumb, from *The Monkey Wrench Gang* by Edward Abbey, copyright by Dream Garden Press. All rights reserved. Related items are available at *http:www.dreamgarden.com* Bottom: Doug Peacock, Livingston, Montana, 2005 by Andrea Peacock.